T0321568

Political Advocacy for School Librarians:
You Have the Power!

Sandy Schuckett

Your Trusted
Library-to-Classroom Connection.
Books, Magazines, and Online

Dedicated to my parents, Max and Bluma Schuckett, who read to me from the beginning, and to the children and young people of the United States, who will be the winners when they have access to strong school library programs.

Library of Congress Cataloging-in-Publication Data

Schuckett, Sandy.
  Political advocacy for school librarians : you have the power! / by Sandy Schuckett.
    p. cm.
  Includes bibliographical references and index.
  ISBN 1-58683-158-5 (pbk.)
  1. School libraries--Government policy--United States--Citizen participation. 2. Libraries and community--United States. 3. Lobbying--United States. I. Title.
Z675.S3S39 2004
027.8'0973--dc22

                                                    2004004869

Author: Sandy Schuckett

Published by Linworth Publishing, Inc.
480 East Wilson Bridge Road, Suite L
Worthington, Ohio 43085

ISBN: 1-58683-158-5

5 4 3 2 1

Table of Contents

Chapter 6: Success Stories

Appendixes

Works Cited

Further Reading

Index

About the Author

Acknowledgments

In this life, little is accomplished alone, and this book would not have been at all possible without the help of a number of people whose assistance and support made it all come together. From long-time California friends and from a simple request on a national school library listserv came a multitude of responses describing proactive advocacy experiences and events throughout the nation.

I would like to thank these diligent school library professionals, paraprofessionals, and supporters for their expertise, their willingness to share information, and their editorial contributions which gave this book its national flavor:

From the ALA Washington Office, Mary Costabile and Emily Sheketoff; from Arizona, Judi Moreillon; from California, Jeff Frost, Megan Fuller, Barbara Jeffus, Linda Jewett, Richard Moore, and Roz Sudakow; from Iowa, Wendy Ziegler; from Minnesota, Doug Johnson; from Missouri, Judy Daniel, Barbara Diment, and Floyd Pentlin; from the National Commission on Libraries and Information Science, Bob Willard; from New York, Carolyn Giambra; from Ohio, Deb Logan and Lynda Murray; from North Carolina, Debbie Hargett; from Pennsylvania, Cathi Fuhrman; from Texas, Cherry Fuller, Janice Richardson, and Jerilynn Williams; from Washington, Marie-Anne Harkness; and from Wisconsin, Neah Lohr and Donna Steffan. Please forgive me if I have inadvertently omitted anyone else who helped.

I would also like to thank the many unnamed dogged and persistent hard workers who keep their state school library associations' Web sites up to date, especially those who include information on advocacy and legislative issues. These Web sites were most helpful in the compilation of information for this book.

And finally, I would like to thank my editor at Linworth, Donna Miller, who convinced this impulsive, right-brain-oriented, somewhat impetuous writer to get organized and "just do it!" Thank you Donna, for your patience, good counsel, understanding, and a BIG PUSH whenever it was needed.

"Never doubt that a small group of thoughtful, committed people can change the world. Indeed, it is the only thing that ever has."

- Margaret Mead, *Coming of Age in Samoa*, 1928

Introduction

A Google search using the keywords "school libraries" + "advocacy" resulted in 6,590 hits; and using the keywords (without the quotation marks or commas) "school libraries" + "politics," "school libraries" + "history," and "school libraries" + "legislation" garnered similar results. After perusing many of the hits and reading information from several of the 50 states, one realizes that school libraries still need help, even though positive outcomes have occurred throughout the country. The positive outcomes have usually been the result of strong and well-organized political advocacy by library media specialists, in collaboration with school administrators, parents, teachers, students, publishers, vendors, and the community at large.

Here are some examples of gains that have been made and work yet to be done:

Maryland, 1998: "*School library funds*–(1) In this subsection, 'new local school board funds means additional funding provided by the local school boards for elementary school libraries in excess of the fiscal 1998 funding provided by the local school boards for elementary school libraries . . . (5) The State Superintendent shall establish guidelines and criteria for the expenditure of funds under this subsection. In developing guidelines, priority shall be given to updating library book and other resource collections" ("House Bill 434" n. pag.).

Iowa, 2001: "It is important for all school library media specialists to become active participants in the lobbying efforts to reinstate the requirement for school library media specialists back into the *Code of Iowa* . . . The following resources have been developed to assist you in your lobbying efforts. Please note that these pre-made letters are not intended to be used verbatim, so please feel free to modify" ("Legislative Issues" n. pag.).

New Mexico, April 18, 2002: "HJM 54 Public School Library Materials was heard by the House Education Subcommittee and received a 'do pass' recommendation. They were unable to act on it before the session ended . . . Introduce (again) a Memorial in the State Legislature to have library materials funded from the same line in the state education budget as textbooks. It was introduced this year, but never reached a vote as the session ended. The goal is one book per student" ("General Membership Meeting" n. pag.).

Kansas, November, 2002: "SCHOOL FINANCE LEGISLATION is a major concern. More than significant cuts are expected . . . We need to lobby heavily for a tax increase to fund K-12 education. Non-mandated programs are always considered for cuts. If school budgets are cut, school library programs are cut" ("Current Legislation and Regulation Issues" n. pag.).

Massachusetts, December, 2002: "Massachusetts education policy makers are not supporting the power of school library media centers to help students achieve. There is great inequity in access to quality literature, information, and library professionals in schools throughout the state . . . The MA Department of Education has no administrator designated to provide leadership and set standards for school library media programs statewide. Neither MA education reform legislation nor the MA Board of Education provides specific funding, leadership, or plans for improving public school library media services. The progressive decay of library media programs in many MA schools has compromised the success of education reform" ("Legislation" Massachusetts n. pag.).

Colorado, 2002: "The State Grants for Libraries Act (SB00-85) was passed and signed into law in 2000. Since then, this act has provided needed educational materials for more than 290 school, public, and academic libraries annually . . . In 2002, because of an anticipated shortfall in state revenues, funding for State Grants to Libraries program was eliminated. Enabling legislation remains on the books, but no money to purchase resources is available" ("The Impact of State Funding for Libraries" n. pag.).

Indiana, 2002: "The second portion of the reading initiative that relates to early reading, the School Library Printed Materials Grant, provides a dollar for dollar match to local school corporations to update school libraries and purchase new books. The goal of the original 1997 portion was to purchase two books per student per year. The grant program grew from $4 million for the 1997-1999 biennium to $6 million for 2001-2003. Nearly 226,000 books were purchased by the fall of 2002" ("Improving School Libraries" n. pag.).

California, 2003: "You saved the Public School Library Act line item last year with your phone calls, letters, and visits detailing why we need to be a separate and distinct line item. We need to do it again! Come back and check the CSLA Web site regularly for alerts on what other action is needed. The students of California are depending on you" ("Legislation" California n. pag.).

Texas, 2003: "The Texas Education Agency has included funding in the amount of 30 cents per student for school library materials through Rider 62 in its Legislative Appropriations Request for 2004-2005. The funding source for this program is available federal and state discretionary funds. However, given recent budget reductions, it is unlikely TEA will have sufficient unexpended federal or state discretionary funds to cover the cost of this program" ("Texas Library Association" n. pag.).

. . . and finally,

South Carolina, 1927: "In 1904 a library act was passed which resulted in the establishment of small book collections in some rural schools. The salient feature of this act 'to encourage the establishment of libraries in the public schools of the rural districts' was the provision of an appropriation of $5,000 annually by the state to be offered in small amounts to schools raising an equal amount, which, in turn, must be met by a third like sum from the county board of the applying school . . . The law is still on the statute books but it is inoperative. Since 1927 there has been no state appropriation to support it" ("The Libraries of South Carolina" n. pag.).

It seems the more things change, the more they stay the same. The quotes reflected above, and many more, show that for some reason school libraries and the people committed to their excellence in providing the best for students and teachers have had a constant struggle in the area of securing funding for materials and staffing. Even though several studies since the 1960s have pointed to the connection between strong school library programs and higher student achievement, the powers that be on local, state, and national levels still just do not seem to get it. Strong grass roots advocacy on the part of library media specialists and their friends and supporters has always played an important part in whatever successes have been achieved. Even during crucial budget deficits and other bad times strong school library advocacy has often prevented funding from being obliterated altogether.

The purpose of *Political Advocacy for School Librarians: You Have the Power!* is to empower school librarians and their colleagues within the school community (and the larger community) to become leaders in advocating for school libraries in the political arena on local, state, and national levels. (Note: The term "librarians" or "school librarians" will be used throughout this book to denote professionals who hold a specific school library certificate or credential. This will include library media specialists, library media teachers, library media coordinators, library teachers, teacher-librarians, or whatever other term a particular state education agency, school district, or school uses for these professional educators.)

Chapter 1 covers the rationale for getting political, and explains why political advocacy is essential in today's climate in the state houses of the nation and in Washington, DC. Chapter 2 helps to remove the mystique from the targets of advocacy: school board members and local, state, and national legislators, and provides tips for establishing good relationships with them. Chapter 3 discusses the message: how to create strong messages using current research as significant ammunition, how to create good sound bites, and how to formulate the answers to tough questions. Chapter 4 provides tips on delivering the message, including how to write lobbying letters, how to speak before boards and committees, and how to be comfortable when meeting legislators or their staff people in person. Chapter 5 covers participation in library legislative days on the federal, state, and local level, what to expect, and how to enjoy the experience. Chapter 6 presents some success stories from colleagues around the country, which will show how leaders in the advocacy effort accomplished notable results by working through their schools, school districts, local and state teachers' associations, state school library associations, and state departments of education, and how technology presented itself as a helpful tool.

Political advocacy works. You have the power. Use it!

Why Listen to Me?

I voted for the President of the United States at the age of five. The year was 1942, we were at war, and on Election Day in early November my dad took me into the voting booth with him. I already knew how to recognize the letters of the alphabet, and using the small rubber "X" stamp, I followed my dad's instructions and placed the stamp first on the inkpad, and then "next to the name that begins with the letter 'R'" on the paper ballot. This simple act was the beginning of the making of a true "political junkie."

I was fortunate to grow up in a home where the issues of the day were constantly discussed at the dinner table. I had involved parents who read up on the issues, joined organizations, wrote letters, made phone calls, always voted, and felt that their voice counted when things needed to be changed. Political involvement and awareness was a way of life for our family. When I attended elementary school, I was also lucky to have several teachers who reinforced and enhanced what I was learning at home. Louise Budde, my fourth grade teacher, taught me to read carefully, loudly, and clearly. Faith Pascal, my fifth grade teacher, ran her classroom like a democracy. We voted on everything! We discussed, and discussed, and discussed. She taught us to listen, to think, to evaluate ideas, and to look for more information when we needed it. Juanita Parks in junior high school made us learn lists and lists of new vocabulary words. And Mrs. Wright (whose first name I have forgotten) was a stickler for correct writing. She even deducted points for every missing or misplaced comma!

Skip to 1978 when I was elected to be one of the 31 California delegates to the first White House Conference on Library and Information Services (WHCLIS) to be held in 1979 in Washington, DC. It was at this conference that

I learned of the tremendous power that grass roots advocacy could have in the ongoing struggle for support for all types of libraries. I had the good fortune to meet two people who had an enormous influence on the direction my life would take, and who both became my mentors. One was Bessie Boehm Moore from Little Rock, Arkansas, who epitomized for me what political action was all about. I watched her like a hawk, and ate up every word she said. I learned how to tell good stories, and how to not be intimidated by lawmakers, since they were just regular people. The other was Eileen Cooke, who was, at the time, the Director of the Washington Office of the American Library Association (ALA), and who taught us, step-by-step, how to make legislators aware of our issues, and how to persuade them to support the things we wanted. I owe a huge debt of gratitude to these two incredible women, who, sadly, are no longer with us.

After WHCLIS I, the White House Conference on Library and Information Services Taskforce (WHCLIST) was created. The Taskforce was composed of two delegates who were elected from each state's WHCLIS delegation in Washington, and its charge was to monitor the actions on the resolutions passed by WHCLIS. We agreed to meet annually, starting in 1980, in a different section of the country. At these meetings, my California colleague, a retired school administrator, and I, along with delegates from the other 49 states, Puerto Rico, Guam, and the American Indian Nations, learned the nuts and bolts of grass roots lobbying to be used on local, state, and national levels. Each year we had speakers who were experts in this arena, and we learned and practiced techniques, asked questions, and then went home and put into practice what we had learned.

In addition, the ALA began "Library Advocacy Now" training. These advocacy training sessions were held at annual and midwinter conferences, and provided information, resources, and techniques, which could be replicated at home in additional training sessions at state and local conferences, so that a large cadre of politically astute library supporters could be created and nurtured in each state. This training, in turn, led me to become more involved in the California School Library Association (CSLA) and the American Association of School Librarians (AASL), which I felt were the best vehicles for school library advocacy on the state and national levels.

On the local level, I was elected president of the Los Angeles School Library Association (LASLA) twice (ten years apart), and in both cases led advocacy efforts to maintain school librarians' jobs and to garner district funding for school library materials.

In 1992 I was elected CSLA Vice-President/Legislation, and began to seriously put into practice all of the things I had learned as we waged the ongoing struggle for support for school libraries in the state. A few years later, I was appointed Chair of the Legislation Committee of AASL, and soon after that, an Intern on the Committee on Legislation of the ALA.

The combination of being an officer on local, state, and national levels gave me a certain amount of clout, and enabled me to begin presenting sessions on political advocacy at conferences on all levels. As these presentations progressed over the years, I was able to refine them as a result of evaluations and feedback from attendees. Even as this was going on, I was continuing to learn from other people involved in advocacy activities. The lobbyists for ALA, CSLA, and the California Library Association (CLA), were also of invaluable assistance, providing me with information, tips on whom to contact on particular issues, and the best steps to take in specific situations.

The successes that occurred from advocacy efforts in the school district, state, and national arenas have prompted the writing of this book.

In California specifically, school librarians who had been relatively unaware of the power they had began attending conference sessions on advocacy. They realized that sitting around and complaining or whining did not accomplish anything, and instead they began to put that energy into writing letters, making phone calls, and visiting legislators. I was able to provide school library colleagues with advice along the way, sample letters to use as writing prompts, or bulleted lists of the major points of a specific message each time action was needed. The advent of technology made it all so much quicker, easier, and more efficient. In the mid 90s listservs were established, both in California and through AASL, so information could be disseminated immediately when action was needed. Listservs continue to be of incalculable value on local, state, and national levels.

Through the 1990s, California school library media folk were becoming more and more politically astute, and by 1998 the combination of that growing political acumen and a huge budget surplus on the state level made the passage of the California Public School Library Act of 1998 possible. The Act provided a distinct and separate line item in the annual state budget specifically dedicated to funding for school library materials and technology, and it was funded at $158.5 million, or $28 per student. This specific line item in the state budget was a huge boon for a state that had been 50th in state school library support ever since statistics had begun to be collected, and this success happened because of grass roots political advocacy on the part of school library people. Further, when the Act was threatened with extinction in 2003, California school librarians again came to the fore, and the line item, though reduced by 95% due to a huge state budget deficit, was maintained.

On the national level, I had the opportunity to work closely with the ALA Washington Office in helping to achieve the passage of the Improving Literacy Through School Libraries Program (the Jack Reed [D-RI] amendment, with co-sponsor Thad Cochran [R-MS]) which became a section of the Elementary and Secondary Education Act (ESEA) Reauthorization in December, 2001. Although the language of the amendment provides for an authorization of $250 million dollars for school library materials and additional training of library media specialists, only $12.5 million in funding was approved by Congress in 2002. Again, technology helped through the AASLFORUM listserv. I was able to provide information when specific action was needed, and school library media supporters throughout the country contacted their U.S. Congressional Representatives and Senators urging them to support this important piece of legislation. Nevertheless, because of the current low appropriation, there is yet more work to be done.

So . . . why listen to me? Twenty-five years of experience in the political arena, with several successes and with the help of brilliant mentors, knowledgeable colleagues, astute library lobbyists, and, above all, building-level librarians who listened and made the choice to act have proven to me that knowing what to do, knowing how to do it, and then doing it really works.

I offer this book as a model for readers to use and adapt as you seek to grow into politically active advocates for strong school library programs.

(Note: Throughout this book there will be references to Web sites on the Internet. At the time of publication, all of these links were functional. However, due to the dynamic and sometimes volatile nature of the Internet, URLs and the information contained on various Web sites is subject to change. Therefore the reader's understanding and indulgence is requested.)

1

Why Politics? Why Lobbying?

Webster's New World College Dictionary defines politics as "the science and art of political government," and "the conducting of or participation in political affairs, often as a profession" (among others); and lobbying as "an attempt to influence a public official in favor of something" . . . "after the practice of meeting with legislators in the LOBBY" ("Politics," def.). For history buffs, it was the lobby of the Willard Hotel, located on Pennsylvania Avenue between the White House and the Capitol in Washington, DC where, in the early part of the twentieth century, the movers and shakers gathered to meet with congressmen and senators to discuss relevant issues.

Traditionally, regular people never got involved in such endeavors. Organizations hired full-time professional lobbyists, often at high costs, to make their members' wishes and desires known to legislators, and to convince the legislators why it was necessary for them to support or defeat a given piece of pending legislation. Successful lobbyists made it their business to know everything there was to know about individual public officials and their staff members. Lobbyists knew how to approach each one, which types of arguments worked and which did not, and how people in decision-making positions responded to messages from constituents. Above all, they knew the value of establishing friendly relationships with legislators and their staffs.

The Internet School Library Media Center (ISLMC) School Library History page <http://falcon.jmu.edu/~ramseyil/libhistory.htm> provides an overview of the development of school libraries in the United States—as an outgrowth of public libraries serving students. The first landmark model legislation for the establishment of school libraries was passed in New York in 1892, and as the twentieth century began, more and more school libraries began to emerge in states throughout the nation. In 1914 the ALA created the School Library section, and in 1920 ALA published the first standards for secondary school libraries. In 1930 ALA published The Program for Elementary School Library Service.

As time passed, through the Post-World War II era, more and more publications emerged, and by 1960 *Standards for School Library Programs* by the American Association of School Librarians in collaboration with the American Association of Colleges for Teacher Education was published by ALA. It was not until 1965, with the passage of the Elementary and Secondary Education Act (ESEA) Title II that federal legislation was firmly in place to provide funding for materials for school libraries throughout the nation. In 1974, ESEA Title IV was created, which consolidated school library funds along with testing plus counseling and guidance, and the strength of the original Act became diluted, as administrators in many places opted to hire additional counselors instead of spending the funds on school library materials.

The 1979 White House Conference on Library and Information Services, the largest White House Conference to that date, was a major impetus for encouraging librarians and library users from all types of libraries to become more involved in the political process on behalf of their libraries, and the focus for those involved with school libraries was to specifically earmark ESEA funding rather than have it continue as a consolidated grant to states. The different speeches and programs at the 1979 conference made it very clear that grass roots advocacy was the only way to garner support for libraries of all types on local, state, and national levels. Delegates learned that a team approach that utilized the expertise of librarians along with the desires of library users for optimum services had the greatest promise of success. The conference provided information, techniques, advice from the professional lobbyists in the ALA Washington Office, and suggestions for activating grass roots advocacy at home.

Viewing the Democratic and Republican political conventions on television in the summer of 2000 reinforced this notion: watching various guests' speaking styles, methods of delivery, the points they emphasized and those they ignored, and the audience members' reactions was truly a political education–and very valuable.

One word that was almost entirely missing from both conventions was the word "library." Only two speakers mentioned this word: Jesse Jackson recalled how, as a young man, he was denied entrance to the public library in his home town in South Carolina, and Susan Bass Levin, who was running for Congress in New Jersey remembered that her dad took her to the public library when she was a small child. None of the speakers mentioned school libraries at all. The speakers addressed various issues with great passion–health care, taxes, working families, and even education reform. How wonderful it would have been to hear the same passion addressed to the need for strong school library programs. It became evident in listening to the major platform planks of each party, as related to education, that school libraries fit into every plank: high standards, accountability, good teachers, safe schools, or family/business/community involvement in local school affairs. It was this last idea of enlarged involvement in schools that brought to my mind the phrase, "Activate for Advocacy."

What does it mean to Activate for Advocacy? This is not a new or unique idea. Many segments of the population have been doing this for years, in both proactive and reactive ways in order to get elected officials to comply with their requests. For school library folk it means that we need to toot our own horns and to work as proactively as possible in assuring that parents, teachers, business owners, and other community members become our strongest allies in reminding legislators that strong school library programs are at the heart of any successful education endeavor. We now have an abundance of recent research to support our position on the need for adequate school library funding. Here is what needs to be done:

- Plug into demands parents have for schools: Produce kids who are good readers. Produce kids who can use technology. Use these two points as inroads to enlist parents' help in political action for school libraries. Parents can become your most powerful allies and they can create an enormous interest in strong school libraries.

- Emphasize your school library program's alignment with curriculum. Show how your program fits into local school priorities, district requirements, state standards and frameworks, and any national standards that are created in all curricular areas. It is important for you to know what these standards are, and how the library fits in; and this information must be transmitted to parents also.

- Emphasize what students need for life-long success: basic literacy, technology literacy, and information literacy. Make it very clear that the school library provides the place, the resources, the skills, and the expertise of a professional, which can help kids to become literate in these three areas.

- Include a specific goal in all advocacy efforts. Is it a specific amount of money-per-student for library materials or technology? Is it professional staffing–one professional library media specialist for every x-number of students? Is it adequate clerical or paraprofessional help in the library? Is it the creation of a school library coordinator position at the state level? Whatever the needs of your community, they must be specified clearly so that all members of the advocacy team are "on the same page" in all advocacy efforts.

As a school librarian, you have the opportunity to become a leader in the advocacy effort because you have a connection to every teacher and student in the school. Excellent programs in your library provide opportunities to meet and work with parents. You might also try to give presentations at PTA meetings and special events, or at local philanthropic organizations such as Rotary, Lions, Moose, Elks or other community clubs. Establish relationships with your principal and with other district administrators, and constantly provide information about your library program and its connection with literacy and with the curriculum. Keep school libraries always on the mind of all decision makers so that when specific issues arise those same decision makers will be more apt to be aware of the necessity for strong school library programs. Use your expertise in technology to improve communication among your colleagues and with your allies in disseminating information when it is needed. Make Activating for Advocacy an ongoing practice–as much a part of your job as ordering books or designing instruction for students, and learn many of the techniques that professional lobbyists use. Lastly, become a leader who can influence the future of school libraries in your school district and your state.

Tips You Can Use Now

■ **Meet** with your colleagues locally and brainstorm to determine which other entities in your community you need to "Activate for Advocacy." Include the existing community activists (every community has them) and enlist their help in working for your goals. Input from your colleagues can help to identify exactly who these people are and how to contact them.

■ **Make** a connection with the leadership of your local and state PTA groups. Offer to be on the agenda for a meeting to speak about school library issues.

■ **Make** a list of local community groups who meet regularly or have special events. Assign the task of obtaining their schedules to one of your colleagues. Obtain commitments from your colleagues to personally contact one or more of the groups you have identified and arrange to speak to them about the specific school library issues that affect their children. Make a "who will do what by when" list and follow through on it.

■ **Decide** on the major message for your school community. This message and the sound bites that go with it will convince everyone on the advocacy team that students need fully staffed and fully supported school libraries. Parents and community members can use this message when they contact decision makers with their requests and demands.

■ **Create** a one-page, bulleted fact sheet that clearly shows the current state of school libraries in your community and what is specifically needed to bring them up to the high standards that students deserve.

2

Who Are the Targets?

Depending on the particular situation, the targets for school library advocacy are many and varied. The most immediate targets could be the teachers and principal of your own school. Or, with the advent of site-based decision making, the local school leadership council might be the target, since this group often decides how money is spent at your school. When specific funding issues arise, does your library automatically get funded, or do you have to grovel and beg to get some paltry pittance? Perhaps in your case the target is the local school board. Do you know the history of school library funding in your school district? Are all of the school board members aware of the library programs in the district? Have they ever visited your library? In many cases, the targets are state or federal legislators. These are elected decision makers who control big purse strings, and their decisions can positively (or negatively) affect how many books or how much current technology your school library has, or even whether or not you get to keep your library clerk or even your own job!

Knowing the Decision Makers

Here's a little quiz: Place a check mark next to every one of these activities in which you, personally, frequently or regularly participate:

- ○ Work hard
- ○ Try to please your students
- ○ Enjoy baseball games
- ○ Watch "Jeopardy"
- ○ Talk a lot
- ○ Buy gifts for your kids, family, friends, and staff
- ○ Visit your local public library
- ○ Surf the Internet
- ○ Get angry
- ○ Tell jokes
- ○ Care about your parents
- ○ Go on diets
- ○ Watch re-runs of *Saturday Night Live*
- ○ Work in the garden
- ○ Worry when your kids are sick
- ○ Cry
- ○ Love your family

The list could go on and on. How many items did you check? Now think about the targets of your advocacy efforts. The bottom-line reality is that principals, school board members, and all legislators, be they local, state, or national, are real people. If you were to give this quiz to them, it is likely that they would check many of the same items you did. Thus there should be no real mystique about them—except for the fact that they have either been appointed or elected to decision-making positions.

As professional lobbyists know, you can achieve greater success in your lobbying efforts if you know something about your legislators or other decision makers. Accomplishing this only requires some research, and school library folks are certainly good at that! With the advent of technology and the Internet, it is now easier than ever to find out about the people who make the decisions. Almost all local, state, and national elected officials have their own Web sites, which might include information on where they were born, what their hobbies are, what issues interest them, who supported their election campaigns, the ethnic make-up of their districts, which community groups they belong to, and what positions of leadership they may hold on state or federal legislative committees.

Finding information about U.S. Congress representatives and senators is also very easy. Each member has a Web site. For Congress, go to <www.house.gov>, and for the U.S. Senate, go to <www.senate.gov>. At each of these gateway sites you can search by zip code or by the member's name and access the congress member's or senator's personal Web site. At the site you will find a variety of information. A biography is usually included, along with a list of the committees on which they are members, information about specific legislation they have introduced, and often press releases of their recent activities. Almost all of the legislators' sites have a variety of photos, in case you do not know what they look like. You might even decide to invite them to your library, take a few photos, and then suggest that one of those photos be put on their Web site! In addition, the addresses and phone numbers of legislators' Washington, DC and local district offices are shown, and there is also a direct link if you want to contact them via e-mail. Although in the early days of electronic communication many legislators were reluctant to accept e-mail messages, that has changed somewhat, and today most of them have staff members whose sole job is to read and respond to e-mail. Most members will only accept e-mail from people who are their constituents, but there are some who have instructed their staff people to read everything that is received.

On the state and local level most legislators and school board members also have their own Web sites. Finding him or her is unique in each district or state, but simple Internet searches almost always work. The information on the Web site is similar to that on the sites of federal legislators.

Establishing Relationships

Why is this information important and how can it be used? Suppose that you find from your research that your congressional representative is interested in the arts, and has authored legislation for funding for the arts? The next time you read an interesting article dealing with the arts why not make a copy of it and send it to her? You will be making a couple of points: 1) as a librarian you are all about providing information on any subject; 2) you care enough about their interest to send them information they might find interesting, helpful, or useful. Make no mistake; they will remember you—especially if you send relevant materials to them more than once.

Another thing that is very important is to read the local papers. They often contain articles about legislators, school board members, or other decision makers. Maybe your local board member participated in a charity golf tournament. How cool would it be if, the next time you got a new book about golf, you took it to his office? You could remind him that you were able to purchase this book because of his support for school libraries, and of course you would also remind him of the due date. Picking up the book would give you another opportunity to visit the office, and another opportunity to talk with him about your library.

Some years ago, in California, there was a very influential state senator whose support we needed. She was the chair of a major education budget committee, and we needed her committee's vote in favor of pending school library legislation. On a visit to her office in the state capitol on Library Legislative Day, we noticed that she had a freestanding bookcase completely filled with various small figurines of elephants. As we were describing how a school librarian collaborates with a classroom teacher to design instruction, one of the librarians said, "Suppose a kid was doing a report on (pause, pause) elephants . . ." The senator's eyes lit up, and she began to discuss her collection. The uttering of that small phrase turned a tense moment into a friendly encounter, and we became more comfortable in discussing our library issues. Several months later, one of the senator's constituents went to visit her in the local district office, and she brought a brand new 32-page picture book about elephants that she had recently received. She thought the senator might be interested in seeing it. The visit was late on a Friday afternoon, and the senator happened to be babysitting her one-and-a-half-year-old granddaughter—right there in her office! As soon as she saw the book, the senator picked up the little one out of the playpen, sat the baby down on her lap, and began reading the elephant book to her. When she returned to the Capitol the following week, she voted positively on proposed school library legislation and influenced the other members of the budget committee, which she chaired, to fund the bill. This happened because of a personal relationship—and the love of elephants (and grandchildren).

Another school librarian had an interesting experience with her U.S. Representative. His major interest was highways and commerce, and he actually knew little, if anything, about school libraries. She talked frequently with the member's local district staff person, often sent articles or other information related to highways and commerce that she thought the congressman might find interesting, and sent a note of congratulations when he was re-elected. When ESEA was up for reauthorization in 1993, this enterprising school librarian received a phone call from the staff member. Question: how should the congressman vote on ESEA? Answer: Vote yes! Because of the relationship she had established with the staff person and because of her credibility as a school library professional, her opinion was respected enough to influence a vote on an issue about which the congressman did not really know much.

Stories like these are repeated every day. The bottom line is that most legislators really DO want to do the right thing. They are in a difficult, stressful position—especially when times are hard and budgets are tight. They may have their politician-type quirks, but most of them ran for office because of a desire to do good work and to make positive changes. They are human beings who just want to be liked like everyone else. Most of them listen to reason. Most of them can be reached on human levels. Most of them can become supporters of school libraries. You have the power to help to assure that this happens.

Tips You Can Use Now

■ **Make** a commitment to visit the Web sites of your school board members, and your state and federal legislators so that you can begin to learn about them.

■ **Write** down three interesting things you learned about each of them, and commit these to memory so that you can use them in conversation (or a letter) later.

■ **Visit** the local office of your state and federal legislators and introduce yourself to the staff person who has the responsibility for education-related issues. If you're in a rural area, and the local office is too far away, write a short letter introducing yourself. Offer to provide them with information about school libraries.

■ **Consider** the special events that are regularly held in your school or in your library and invite the legislator to attend. You can invite them to make a small speech, to present a special award to a student, to read to kids in the library, to install student body officers, or to do anything else that will create a great "photo op."

■ **Create** an information sheet on your legislative officials for your own use. Keep it handy so you can use it when you need to contact them. Include the following:

- Name
- Local office address and phone number
- State Capitol or Washington, DC office address and phone number
- Specific committees on which they serve
- When their term ends
- Main issues which interest them
- URL for Web site

3

What Is the Message?

One of the most critical pieces of your advocacy effort is to develop a clear, concise, coherent message before you begin contacting legislators or other decision makers. The message must contain significant details pertaining to your specific aims and requests, and it must not contain library jargon. You must be prepared with good sound bites and the answers to tough questions, and you must be very familiar with the research that shows the relationship between strong school libraries and higher student achievement.

Creating the Message Document

It is best to create a message document, which is written in a format that is easily understood. Once written, distribute this document among the members of your advocacy team and then modify it as needed for the decision makers who are your targets.

1. Begin with a clear, concise statement of the specific request: "Action is needed now to support (bill number, issue, etc.)."
2. Include the specific date and place where the issue will be discussed and the decision will be made: "This bill will be heard on (date) in the (board meeting, committee, legislative house.)"
3. Follow up with one or two (at the most) paragraphs, which specify any background material that pertains to your request. For example, if you are asking for an increase in funding for library materials, then you will want to review what the current funding is, what (if any) specific pieces of legislation created the funding, and why the funding must be increased. A good idea is to mention national averages of books-per-student (refer to *Information Power: Building Partnerships for Learning,* ALA, 1998) and compare the figures with those of your school district or state. If you want to attach a page delineating the main findings of the research that has been done in support of school libraries, include a sentence stating that the page is attached.
4. After the background statement, repeat the main goal and the rationale concisely and then add a statement asking for support: "We need your help in supporting strong school library programs for students" or "We need your help in bringing the number of books-per-student in (state's, district's) school libraries up from (x) to (x)."
5. Finally, add a statement specifically setting out what you want the advocate or the public official to do: (Advocate)—"Contact your (board member, legislator) now and urge them to support (bill number.)" (Decision maker)—"We urge you to vote in favor of (bill number), which will provide (your district's, your state's) students with the optimum school library services they need and deserve in order to become successful in today's world."

Utilizing Current Research

Whether you are planning a letter-writing campaign, meetings with local business leaders or the PTA, or visits to legislative offices, it is essential that your message emphasize the benefits of strong school library programs for students. One of the best ways to accomplish this is to cite recent research showing that an investment in school libraries is an investment in assuring higher student achievement.

When the first Colorado Study, *The Impact of School Library Media Centers on Academic Achievement* (Lance, 1992), was released, a loud celebration occurred throughout the school library world. Even though we in the field knew that the study's findings were true long before its appearance, it was heartening to see it in black and white. What we knew to be true from our own experience was suddenly validated in a very compelling, empirical way. Another advantage of this publication was an excellent bibliography, which presented references to the major research related to school libraries that had been done from the 1950s through 1989.

Keith Curry Lance's study of school libraries in Colorado was only the beginning of modern school library media research. He and others went on to conduct similar studies in Colorado and in many other states, and each time the results were similar: more support for school libraries leads to students who are better readers, students who perform better on standardized tests, and students who attain a higher level of academic achievement.

Between 1992 and 2003, 13 additional school library media studies were completed: Pennsylvania, 1999; Alaska, 2000; Colorado "2," 2000; Iowa, 2000; Massachusetts, 2000; Minnesota, 2001; Oregon, 2001; Texas, 2001; New Mexico, 2002; Florida, 2003; Michigan, 2003; Missouri, 2003; and North Carolina, 2003. Access to these studies is provided on the Library Research Service's (LRS) Web site at <www.lrs.org>; LRS is a division of the State Library of Colorado, the home base of Lance's work.

After reaching the LRS home page, accessing the individual studies is simple. Click on "School" at the top, then on the next page click on "Impact Studies" at the left. This will bring you to a list of all the states where the studies have been conducted. You can click on any particular state study, and depending upon its format you can access the complete study (usually in PDF format) or an executive summary. In some cases you will find an easily printable "three-fold" brochure, a one page bulleted list of the findings, or even a PowerPoint presentation on the study that can be downloaded. In some cases the whole study is not presented, but information is included showing how to order the study. Purchasing the study is worthwhile, and each study would be a valuable addition to the reference section of any school library.

Use the printouts of the results of any of these school library studies for powerful pieces of ammunition in advocacy efforts; they also provide needed information to parents, teachers, school administrators, and other community members. Attach the printouts to letters or hand them to legislators at hearings or during office visits, and as an advocate point out specific findings that clearly show why investment in school library programs is a necessity for students. It is worth the time needed to explore and print out the brochures or executive summaries of these studies.

ALA and AASL provide another excellent site that presents school library research. If you access the ALA Web site <www.ala.org> and then enter "SLMR" (without the quotation marks) in the "Search" field, the search results will show a large number of different studies and documents related to school library media research. This service is a successor to *School Library Media Quarterly Online,* and its purpose is to "publish high quality original research concerning the management, implementation, and evaluation of school library media programs" ("About SLMR" n. pag.). If you are interested in receiving notification of new research as it is completed and added to SLMR you can add your e-mail address to the SLMR electronic notification list. Send your request directly to Editor Danny Callison at <callison@indiana.edu>.

An additional body of research that presents valuable ammunition in school library advocacy endeavors is that done by Dr. Stephen Krashen, Professor of Education at the University of Southern California in Los Angeles. His book, *The Power of Reading,* presents definitive studies, which show that students who read more read better. Here are some of his conclusions (Krashen, "Notes" n. pag.):

- Voluntary reading is the best predictor of reading comprehension, vocabulary growth, spelling ability, grammatical usage, and writing style.
- Having a library media specialist makes a difference in the amount of voluntary reading done by students.
- Access to school library media centers results in more voluntary reading by students.
- Larger school library collections and longer hours increase both access to curriculum and amount read.

Krashen also includes several very powerful quotes regarding the necessity for well-supported school library programs. The following are a few examples ("Notes" n. pag.):

- "Enriching the print environment by means of a school library results in more reading."
- "Children who had access to school libraries did more reading than children who only had access to centralized book collections (without librarians)."
- "Students take more books out of school libraries that have more books and stay open longer."
- "The richer the print environment, that is, the more reading material available, the better the literacy development."
- "If many students do indeed lack access to books and if the

arguments for reading as the source of literacy development are even partly correct, libraries are crucially important."

At this point in time we are in an excellent position when so many politicians, school district administrators, and others are saying that everything that happens in schools needs to be research based. We have many, many research studies that can be cited, they are easily accessible, and they are just waiting to be used by leaders in the advocacy effort.

Creating Good Sound Bites

In today's fast moving, high-tech climate it seems that the sound bite has become the major method of communication. This is true in the marketplace where advertising must make its point quickly and potently and it is true in the political arena where candidates and proponents of specific issues must do the same. Everyone is busy, and unfortunately, no one wants to spend a lot of time reading lengthy treatises related to any specific issue.

Whether you are preparing message documents, planning for an address before a school board or a legislative committee, writing a letter to the editor of your local newspaper, or suddenly have a microphone thrust in front of you at a major event, make sure to have in mind a few well-rehearsed sound bites. Try to work sound bites into a conversation no matter what specific school library issue you discuss.

Also, there may be an occasion (a rally for libraries or education, or a library legislative day in your state capitol) where large buttons displaying a forceful sound bite can be very effective. Several years ago, such a rally was held at the headquarters of a large urban school district in California when budget cuts threatened many certificated positions including librarians, nurses, counselors, and others who were not classroom teachers. The school nurses attended en masse, and all wore large buttons, three or four inches in diameter, which showed a large red "drop," and carried the slogan, "When nurses are cut, children bleed." At the actual board meeting where the budget cuts were discussed and decided, more than 50 school librarians attended, and all wore shocking pink T-shirts with lettering, which said, "Don't shelve librarians." Several nurses and librarians spoke before the board, as well as parents, students, and teachers, and after each address the respective group stood up, cheered and applauded, and provided a very powerful visual/verbal statement, which was also shown on television. It was very compelling. When the school board finally voted, funding for both school librarians and nurses was not cut!

The best sound bites are short, catchy, and clever; and they stress the major point you are trying to make. Some examples of good sound bytes collected from various people and sources follow:

- The road to academic achievement leads directly through the school library.
- Libraries are a school's information infrastructure.
- If we did not already have school libraries, we would have to invent them.
- Kids who read succeed.
- The school library is the most cost-effective classroom in the school.
- The more you read, the more you know.
- Readers are leaders.
- If you need to know, go to your school library.
- Good decisions depend on good information.
- When in doubt, ask a librarian.

Think of advertising slogans that remain in your mind, and try to figure out why they are so catchy. As an exercise, see how many school library sound bites you can write. If you can make them pertain to your specific school, district, or state, so much the better. This would also be a good activity for a meeting with your colleagues or with your advocacy team. Like any writing, the more you do it, the easier it becomes. You might even want to present this as an activity for middle or high school students. You will probably not be surprised at some of the brilliant and creative sound bites that your students will produce. Having a store of good sound bites ready to use for any advocacy campaign is an advantage, and choosing a specific one as the slogan for a particular endeavor can only make your position stronger.

Answering Tough Questions

As you become a proactive leader in the school library advocacy arena, you will be confronted with tough questions at some point. These might come from parents, teachers, school administrators, other community members, or legislators themselves. It is best to be prepared. Most questions arise from people who remember their own school libraries from fifty years ago and think that all librarians do is stamp books, which was not even true then; or, they can arise from parents who are genuinely concerned about what their children see on the Internet. There are also those who really believe that the Internet can replace libraries and librarians altogether, and those legislators who, in the interest of saving money, think it would be a good idea for public libraries to take over the tasks that school libraries now perform.

There is a right way and a wrong way to respond to tough questions. It does not matter who is doing the asking. The most important point is to always answer with a positive rather than a negative, and to emphasize the benefits for students. Coming across as if you are on the defensive is a bad idea! The object of the answer is to provide the correct information, and to make the points that need to be heard. So, for example, if the question is: "In these tough budget times, why should we take money from prisons or AIDS research and give it to school libraries?" the wrong answer would be: "We're not taking money from prisons or AIDS research." A better answer would be: "We feel that education is a large part of the solution to problems such as AIDS and criminal behavior. Students who have access to current and correct information in their school library will be better equipped to make better choices in their lives. Money spent on prevention now means less money will be needed to 'fix' problems later. Spending money on school libraries now is simply a good investment in the future."

As an advocate you can make your strongest points with prepared answers to tough questions. Here are some sample questions and appropriate answers:

Q: What is information literacy?

A: Information literacy is a critical skill in today's world. It is the ability to find the right information to solve a particular problem and the ability to evaluate information to determine if it is authoritative and accurate. It is the ability to know when to use books and when to use electronic means.

Q: Why does a school need a librarian when everything is on computers? Kids can just look up books in the catalog and check them out themselves.

A: The school librarian is a teacher who instructs students in the skills they need to find and use information to complete school assignments or for their own use or enjoyment. The librarian knows the school curriculum and knows how the materials in the library can be plugged into it. The librarian knows the students and knows the library's collection, and is an expert at joining the two together.

Q: If school libraries are in such need, why do they throw away books? Why do they turn down my donations of my old books, and especially my last 25 years of National Geographic?

A: School librarians are most appreciative of donations by parents, friends, and other community members. However, the main purpose of the school library collection is to supplement the curriculum. Librarians have very specific standards and policies related to what goes on library shelves. The materials must be on the appropriate level; they must be current; they must be related to the curriculum; they must be items that have been well reviewed by professional journals; and they must be free of biased points of view or stereotypes. In order to keep the collection current it is often necessary to discard older materials when new ones on the same subject become available. We do not want our students to read outdated or inaccurate scientific material or to do research on countries that no longer exist. Children deserve only the latest and the best in school library books.

Q: Why will you not tell parents what books their kids have checked out?

A: All materials in our school library have been evaluated and chosen following a very definite selection policy, and we believe they are appropriate for the students in this school. We respect each library user's privacy, and we feel that passing on information about what students are reading would be a breach of this privacy. We believe that parents and students together must decide what materials the students may or may not read.

Q: How is the Internet being used in your school library? Isn't there stuff on the Internet that kids in schools should not see?

A: Our (school, district) has a very definite policy concerning the use of the Internet which all students and their parents are required to sign at the beginning of each school year. We have bookmarked specific sites that are available to assist students in completing research for their school projects. We monitor students' Internet use carefully, assuring that they are "on task" with their research activities. Since many students need to use library computers, students are learning to find what they need quickly, thereby freeing up the computer for another student who is waiting. (Or, if your school library computers are filtered, say so.)

Q: Why do we need a school library if we have a children's room at the public library?

A: Both types of libraries are important to all children in the community. The school library is a resource-filled classroom where the collection is geared to the curriculum and the librarian collaborates with the classroom teacher to provide instruction in the lifelong skills of finding and using information that every child needs in order to be successful in the future. The materials are available during the entire school day, and can be accessed immediately at point of need. The public library provides a wide variety of additional materials and after-school, weekend, and vacation programs for the child's enjoyment and learning.

Other techniques are helpful when a questioner puts you on the spot. The first is to remain calm, smile, think, and then respond. It is OK to pause for a few seconds. This shows that you are a thoughtful person, and not one who impulsively blurts out an answer. You can also use the question as a "bridge" to another point you want to make, or to a good (but short) story that illustrates your point. For example, after answering the question about the use of the Internet, you might give a quick example of a student who found exactly what he needed for use in a school project. You could be asked a question that has a built-in negative. "Isn't it true that school librarians just check out books all day?" Answer it quickly, and then bridge to the real points you want to make: "That may have been true in the past; however, today's school librarians . . . (and then elaborate.)"

A good way to emphasize your points while answering questions is to add phrases such as, "The more important thing about this is . . ." or "There are three answers to your question. The first is . . ." or "I am so glad you asked that question. As you can appreciate, . . ."

During local and national election campaigns listen carefully to candidates as they respond to questions from the press. Candidates have been trained to be "media savvy," and you can learn a lot by watching the way they answer the tough questions.

Tips You Can Use Now

■ **Create** a message document related to your school library issues following the five points outlined earlier in this chapter, and share it with your colleagues. Get their input and revise it to make it as clear and as strong as possible.

■ **Assign** a few of the members of your advocacy team the task of printing out the executive summaries or brochures of the school library impact studies from the Library Research Service Web site. Compile these into a file that can be used whenever you need it.

■ **Explore** businesses in your community that have the capability of making large buttons. Obtain estimates of the prices and production time, and keep this information handy for later use. After you have created a specific sound bite targeted toward a particular issue, ask a colleague or an artistic student to design a button, and save this for later use also.

■ **Brainstorm** with colleagues to come up with additional tough questions that might be related to particular issues in your own community. Then brainstorm the answers and decide on the best way to answer each one, remembering to always be positive and to always emphasize what is best for students.

■ **Practice** answering tough questions. Do some role-playing with your colleagues or your advocacy team. If you are accustomed to being questioned under pressure you will be better able to respond positively in a relaxed manner when confronted in a real situation.

4

How Do I Deliver the Message?

Now that you have made a commitment to become involved in the political process, decided on the targets of your advocacy efforts, and brainstormed with your colleagues and supporters to create a usable message document, you are ready to learn techniques for delivering the message in the strongest possible manner.

Depending upon the specific situation and the particular issue, there are several ways to deliver your message. You may need a letter writing campaign or visits to your legislators' or other decision makers' local district offices. You may be called upon to speak before a legislative committee or the board of education. Or, you may decide to participate in Library Legislative Day in your state capitol or in Washington, DC. There are skills to be learned as you undertake each of these endeavors.

Writing Effective Letters

Letters or e-mail messages are usually needed when a specific issue is "of the moment." It might be that a particular piece of legislation affecting school libraries is slated for hearing in your state legislature, in the Congress, or in a legislative committee. Your local school district may be threatening cuts of librarians' or library aides' positions or a decrease in funding for school library materials. Perhaps your local newspaper has published an article about the area's schools and has completely omitted any mention of the libraries in the schools, or maybe they misstated information, and it must be corrected. In all of these cases, a well-written letter can be very effective.

It has been said that, especially on the federal level, one letter received by a legislator is equal to approximately 500 people who probably feel the same way but just did not take the time to write. During the debate in the U.S. House of Representatives on the 1993 ESEA reauthorization, one of the issues under discussion was Title III, Part F, a section of ESEA, which would provide a specific authorization for school library materials. One of the members of Congress stood gripping a sheaf of papers in his hand, and said, "I hold here in my hand 50 letters from my constituents extolling the virtues of strong school libraries." He went on to speak on behalf of the School Library Title. When he finished, other members followed him stating their support for the issue. On October 3, 1994, the legislation, HR6, passed, and Title III, Part F was added to the 1993 incarnation of ESEA. Unfortunately Title III, Part F was never funded, so it was removed, along with all other unfunded federal mandates in 1996, but the point still remains: writing a letter is an effective tool.

On the state or local level, one letter is probably equal to fewer than 500 people with a similar opinion, but the fact remains that several short, clear letters still have a definite impact on legislators' decision making.

Writing letters establishes recognition of your name in the decision-maker's office. This is a definite advantage. A simple letter of congratulations when someone is elected or appointed, with an offer to answer any questions they may have related to school libraries, is a good idea. This act immediately suggests that you are knowledgeable in this area; thus you will probably be the one they contact when questions arise.

The main thing to keep in mind when writing lobbying letters is to make them short. One page is best, and absolutely no more than two! Legislators and their staff members receive hundreds of pieces of paper daily, and you do not want them to be immediately turned off when they see that your letter is quite long. Make your points quickly and clearly, and if you are asking the decision makers to do something specific, state that clearly also. If you have created a good message document, you can often "lift" phrases directly from it to your letters.

The first step is to address the recipient properly. With elected officials, it is customary to address them as "The Honorable John Smith," "Assemblymember Susan Jones," "Senator Robert Garcia," or "Representative Mary Williams" on the envelope and in the inside address. In the salutation, repeat their title: "Dear Mr. Smith," "Dear Assemblymember Jones," "Dear Senator Garcia," or "Dear Representative Williams."

Following is a sample of an effective lobbying letter that is easily written in a few sentences:

Date

The Hon. Robert Garcia
_____ State Senate
State Capitol
City, State Zip

Dear Senator Garcia:

(Write one or two sentences identifying yourself and telling them exactly what you want them to do.)

"I am the librarian at XYZ Middle School, and I am writing to urge you to support S1234, the School Libraries Act, which will provide much needed current books and electronic resources for students at my middle school and throughout (state)."

(Write one or two sentences expressing your feelings about the issue and how it will affect your students.)

"At a time when students' reading scores are a big concern, I'm sure you are aware of the important role that strong school libraries play in creating better readers. Our library at XYZ Middle School requires these new books and other resources to assure that our students have access to the latest and best materials to meet their reading and information needs."

(Write one or two sentences asking for a response and offering assistance.)

"Please respond and assure me that I can count on your support of S1234, which will improve school library services for students. I have attached a copy of the conclusions from recent research that shows the connection between well-funded school libraries and raised student achievement, and I would be happy to provide you with additional information on this issue if necessary."

Sincerely,

Your name
Your address
Your phone number
Your e-mail address

Write your letter on personal letterhead if you have it. Many people think that handwritten letters are the best, and if you do write your letter by hand, be sure it is legible! However, a letter typed on a computer is also acceptable. The key is that it must sound original and from the heart, and should not feel like a form letter. The reader needs to feel that your letter comes from a real person who cares deeply about the issue and who truly knows something about it. Avoid phrases that sound trite or clichéd, and never demand anything!

It is also often acceptable to send a fax or an e-mail. At this point in time, most legislators and other decision makers have become quite technologically astute, and if they have not, there is usually someone on their staff who has. The advantage of fax and e-mail is that they are immediate, and this is especially helpful when there is short notice related to an impending decision and there is not enough time to use the U.S. Mail.

Once you have mastered the technique of writing an effective lobbying letter, pass this skill on to your colleagues and other members of your advocacy team. As a leader in the advocacy efforts of your state or school district, launch a letter writing campaign when one is needed, and you will have done your job by assuring that decision makers receive a group of effective letters educating them on the necessity of supporting your issue.

Tips You Can Use Now

■ **When** writing a letter remember that short is best—one or two pages—no more.

■ **State** exactly what you want; be specific; be clear.

■ **Relate** the issue to your particular school or school district; how will it help kids?

■ **Attach** research documents (short) where appropriate.

■ **Fax** or e-mail your letter if the issue is immediate; send "snail mail" copy also if time permits.

Speaking Before Boards and Committees

Very often, in the course of school library life it becomes necessary to speak before your local school board or a legislative or congressional committee about issues that affect your library program. You might be fighting to create, increase, or preserve funding for your library program and materials, or, in a worst-case scenario, to save your positions or those of the paraprofessionals who work with you to create the optimum library program for your students. Although the thought of having to participate in such an activity may seem daunting at first, actually doing it is not difficult. Anyone who stands before classes of kids all day or who provides staff development sessions for their teacher colleagues can be equally effective in front of a school board or a committee whose members are politicians. Imagine that the board or committee members are all third graders, and it will be easy!

Arch Lustberg, the author of *How to Sell Yourself: Winning Techniques for Selling Yourself . . .Your Ideas . . .Your Message* has made a career out of training politicians, business executives, and advocates from all walks of life in the techniques of speaking before boards and committees. He talks about the quality of "likeability"—using your mind, your face, and your body language to convince your listeners that not only is your point of view correct, but that you are a "nice, friendly person" (Lustberg, "Notes" n. pag.).

If you have ever sat in on a meeting of a city council, board of education, or other decision-making body, you have probably heard testimony that would put any sane person to sleep. Often people who are testifying bring prepared remarks, which they then proceed to read . . . droning on and on and on. If you have been bored by such an experience, you can imagine the feelings of the decision makers who have to listen to this type of speech making on a regular basis. The bottom line is that they usually tune it out.

When you speak before such a group, your goals are: 1) be sure they are listening; 2) show that you know what you are talking about; 3) make them like you so they will do what you want them to do. Lustberg talks about the "open face." This is the expression most people use when talking to cute babies or small children: eyebrows raised, eyes wide-open, mouth in a smile. Try it in the mirror! Imagine that you are speaking to your adorable two-year-old nephew or your cuddly little granddaughter. This "open face" is more likely to elicit a positive response on the part of your listeners than a serious, frowning countenance with eyebrows clenched and eyes squinting. Body language is another thing that can either help you or hurt you. It is important to be relaxed. If you know what you are talking about, if you have practiced, and if you truly believe in what you are saying, your body language will reflect this. If you normally use your hands while talking, it is OK to use them when addressing a board or committee—anything that is natural for you works. Use a voice that is strong and clear, and avoid a monotone. Modulate your remarks into louder and softer segments depending on the emphasis that you want to present. Be animated and speak slowly enough so that every word will be heard—again, imagine that you are teaching a class of third graders. Do not forget passion. Your listeners need to know that you really believe in this issue. Noted poet Maya Angelou recently said, remarking on the effectiveness of Martin Luther King, Jr.'s "I Have a Dream" speech, "If you have the language, the passion, and a cause, of course you will be successful" (qtd. on *CBS Evening News*).

In your remarks before a board or a committee it is important to always focus on student results, and emphasize that an investment in good school library programs is an investment in learning. Using charts or graphs or other visuals that highlight specific points or statistics makes a presentation even better. Even bringing a student to hold them up can be effective. Many people are visual learners, and showing a chart breaks up the monotony of just speaking. It is also a good idea to bring a one- or two-page handout that reinforces whatever you are saying, and give it to the members after you speak.

If the experience of speaking before a board is new to you or even if you are an old hand, it is probably a good idea to write out what you plan to say. Be sure that you find out in advance what your time limit will be. Usually you will have no more than three to five minutes. If you are well organized you can squeeze a lot into this seemingly short amount of time. This is where potent phrases, catchy sound bites, and specific pieces of information come into play. Say what you need to say without trying to sound erudite or intellectual. Simple language is best. Use regular words that leave no question as to their meaning. Arch Lustberg has a "popular-but-pompous" list of "no-nos": infrastructure, paradigm, oxymoron, indigenous, erstwhile, parameter ("March" n. pag.). Strike these words and others like them from your speaking vocabulary! Do not use library jargon. Only other librarians know what you are talking about—decision makers do not. Have your message clearly in mind, with emphasis on three, and no more than five, major points. Use facts and figures for emphasis where needed and always focus on benefits for kids. Remember that rambling on does not work. When writing out your remarks, know where to end, and remember that even a windbag does not love another windbag!

One helpful suggestion is to type your remarks in ALL CAPITAL LETTERS, double- or even triple-spaced, using a large font and very wide margins on the left- and right-hand sides of your text. This technique that TV newspeople use makes your presentation easier to read since you can see one or more whole lines at a time, and each word will be visually crystal clear. Using this method of typing your remarks also makes it easier to alternate your line of vision from your notes to the listeners. You can quickly (silently) read an idea, and then state it as you are looking into the faces of the board or committee members. You can also place notes to yourself in the margins such as "emphasize," "use chart," or any other reminders that, under pressure, you might forget. Use highlighters and different colors of pens to write any reminders you think you might need.

Practice your speech using your written pages. Let your family and friends be your guinea pigs as you begin by reading it aloud to them, or lock yourself in the bathroom and read it aloud again and again. If you read your presentation over several times, the words and their flow will become very familiar to you, and you can then just use the paper as a prompt. But do not veer off the text too much, because it will use up your time. Use a timer to be sure your words have not exceeded your time limit. There is nothing more frustrating than speaking before a group and being told that your time is up before you have reached your major point. Trying to rush to squeeze in everything in four or five remaining seconds just comes across as a garbled mess, and you get no points for being convincing. Practicing aloud also allows you to hear how your remarks come across. It may be that you need a bit of rewriting to shorten, clarify, or emphasize a point. When you have practiced and feel comfortable with your presentation you are ready to address the board of education or legislative committee on your school library issues.

When the time comes for you to speak before the board or the committee, enjoy yourself. Be friendly, smile, look at each of the people you are addressing, and reach them on a human level. Since you have practiced sufficiently and know what you are talking about, you will not need to bury your nose in your papers. Be sure you are close enough to the microphone to be heard clearly. Do not be afraid to be passionate. Passion is contagious, and your passionate presentation will get and keep their attention. If you can add humor, do it! All people like to laugh. Tip O'Neill, venerated Speaker of the House from 1977 to 1986, said, "Having a sense of humor is another good principle in political life" (O'Neill xii).

Remember that it often works better if parents, teachers, other community members, or even kids talk about your library program and its advantages for students. If you can recruit someone to speak for you, do so. You can coach them on the speaking techniques mentioned above. If they speak on behalf of your library it does not seem so much like you are begging for support. They are voters and constituents, and board and committee members are likely to listen to them. If possible, invite as many colleagues and other supporters as possible to come and hear your address. It does not hurt to have a cheering section, and this will show the board or committee that many more people have a stake in the issue and feel the same way that you do about it.

When you have finished you will realize that it was not so hard after all. You will feel great about yourself, you will feel empowered, and you will know that your words have had an impact. The more you do it, the easier it gets. Good luck!

Tips You Can Use Now

- **Focus** on student results.

- **Be** concise; be clear; do not ramble; stick to the issue.

- **Practice**, practice, practice!

- **Use** the "open face"; smile; be passionate; relax; have fun!

- **Stay** within the time limit.

- **Bring** your own cheering section.

Meeting with Decision Makers in Person

Face-to-face communication between decision makers and their constituents is often one of the most effective methods of obtaining positive results in advocacy efforts. If you have already established a personal relationship with your legislators or school board members, all the better. You will have name recognition when you call for an appointment or to invite the decision maker to a special event at your school library.

If the person with whom you wish to meet is newly elected or appointed, you have the opportunity to meet them at the beginning of their term, and to begin to educate them and to establish yourself as the school library expert in the area or the district.

Inviting local legislators to an event at your school is one good way to meet them in person. Legislators love to be seen in photos with kids in a local school, so be sure you take plenty of pictures. If the event is in your library you will have the opportunity to show them around, pointing out special collections or programs for students or how technology is used in information literacy instruction. Their visit also gives you a chance to mention some of the kinds of things you could do for students if your program were better supported. One thing that is very effective with legislators is showing them "ugly books," that is, books that need to be weeded because they are outdated, incorrect, or reinforce ethnic or gender stereotypes. Books that say, "Man will some day go to the moon," or "Men build houses; women clean them," or those that show the "happy" slaves singing in the cotton fields are good examples. Most legislators or school board members have no idea that such books still sit on the shelves of many school libraries throughout the country, and they have to agree with you that students should not be using such materials for their pleasure reading or for assigned research projects. Showing them outdated computers or faulty, slow, or non-existent wiring and connectability can also accomplish positive results. All legislators want the students in their districts to have the advantage of the Internet and other up-to-date technology. Another valuable activity is to invite a legislator into your library AFTER you have weeded. Doing this provides a powerful visual experience for them. "Why are the shelves so empty?" he might ask . . . and of course you have the answer. Inviting legislators and board members to your school should be an ongoing activity on your part. The more frequently they are there, the better . . . then, when there is a specific issue where their direct action is needed it will be easier to reach them since they will already have some knowledge of you, your school, your library, and your program.

When there is a specific issue that will require the decision maker's vote or other positive (or occasionally, negative) action, a visit to the local office is in order. As constituents, you, parents, teachers, or students should always be welcome in the local office of a board member or a legislator. After all, your taxes pay their salaries! Your first step is to decide on the best time to schedule the visit.

Your school district probably has a Web site where you can access the schedule of board of education meetings and find addresses and phone numbers for board members' offices. Most of the information provided below related to meeting with legislators can also be used in relation to meeting with school board members or trustees.

Usually, most state-level legislators return to their local districts on Thursday nights, and they are in their local offices on Fridays, so this would be a good time to schedule an appointment. If your state legislative bodies have their own Web sites (most do) you can see their schedule for the whole year. Often there will be long periods of time when they are not in session, depending upon the state, and you can plan to visit their local offices then.

On the federal level, you can access THOMAS—Legislative Information on the Internet at <http://thomas.loc.gov>. Click on "Days in Session Calendar" on the left-hand side. (By the way, this site is named for Thomas Jefferson, and the Library of Congress maintains it.) On the next screen you can choose either the House of Representatives or the Senate, and you will see calendars for the full year, showing red numbers for the dates they are in session. You will note that similar to state level legislative bodies, there are also long periods of time when they are not in session, and chances are that on many of those days legislators will be home in the local district.

Once you have decided when you want to visit the local office you need to call and make an appointment. Most legislative offices have a scheduler whose specific job is to handle appointments. Jot down this person's name for future reference, and initiate an acquaintance with them over the phone. Often schedulers can be your best allies in getting an appointment with legislators. If your school is in session, you will probably want to make the appointment in the late afternoon. Staff members will understand that you do not want to take time away from your job at school to participate in an office visit, and they will generally be quite accommodating to your time request. The scheduler will probably say something like, "I will check with the senator and get back to you." This could take a couple of hours or a couple of days or even longer. Generally, if you have not heard back from them in a week it is a good idea to call again. If you already have name recognition with the legislator, you will be more likely to have an appointment scheduled right away.

Many times the scheduler will say, "The congressman is totally tied up that week, but I could schedule a meeting with the staff person who handles our education issues." Although you would probably prefer to meet with the congressman himself, meeting with staff is fine. In some cases it is even better than meeting with the congressman. A staff person who is exclusively concerned with education issues will have a great deal of background that can be very helpful in your discussions, and you will be amazed at how many of them are lovers of libraries and will begin telling you stories of their school or public library experience as a child or teenager. One congressional staff member in California went into a thirty-minute discussion of his bookmark collection during an office visit with a small group of school librarians! When something like this happens, you just have to sit there and nod and smile and agree that this is all great, and maybe add a word or two about *your* bookmark collection. Then, you can get to the issue at hand. Remember that this staff person is the one who has the congressman's ear. Legislators deal with many, many issues, and there is the possibility that school libraries, or even education itself, may not be their number one interest; it may be medical care, or highways, or bringing big business into the area. Therefore, they rely strongly on the opinions of their staff members, and often make decisions on specific votes depending upon the advice they have received from staff. Additionally, especially on the federal level, it is the staff person who does the bulk of the legislative work. They often draft bills that their bosses carry; they do all the related reading and research, and then synthesize it for the boss; they make connections with other members of congress or the senate when they need co-sponsors or support for particular bills. Establishing a good relationship with an education staff person can often be the strongest "plus" in your advocacy efforts, be they on the local, state, or national level.

There will be times when you feel that you absolutely must meet with the school board member or legislator herself. This could be the case if you have already had one or more meetings with staff. It is OK to politely but firmly insist that this is what you want. You are a constituent, after all, and it does not hurt to remind the scheduler of this—in a very courteous and non-threatening manner. Of course, if you have already established a friendly relationship with the schedulers they will go out of their way to grant your request.

When the appointment is made, your next step is to decide whether you will go to the meeting alone or be accompanied by others. It depends upon the specific issue. Sometimes, if you already have an established relationship with the decision maker, it might be best to go by yourself for a short meeting where you will quickly discuss the issues at hand, let him know what you want him to do, and then leave. If the purpose of your visit is to educate the legislator on a broad range of library issues, you might want to bring others with you. Usually a group of three or four people is large enough. You might want to bring a teacher, a parent, and a student, or, you might want to bring a couple of colleagues from different schools in the legislator's district. Again, it depends upon what your issues are and what you are trying to accomplish.

You also need to decide what to bring on the visit. If your goal is to garner support for a specific bill or resolution, then you will want to bring your message document that you have already adapted specifically for that legislator (see chapter 3). Perhaps you will want to create a one-page, bulleted sheet stating your wishes and the reasons why they are necessary for students. If it is to be a purely educational visit, you might want to bring copies of the executive summaries of the library studies, (see chapter 3), or it might be a good idea to bring some examples of something that was made by kids as a result of a wonderful activity that they experienced in their school library. Legislators generally love to receive things made by kids. In one state, students wrote and illustrated letters about favorite new books that were purchased with state library funds, and these were presented to state legislators, some of whom even framed a couple of them for the office wall! Students at all levels all over the United States are producing excellent projects related to books and other materials they have accessed through their school libraries that encompass the many information literacy skills they are learning. The people who hold the purse strings and make the decisions need to see these projects! Maybe a group of students has created an original CD-ROM related to life in ancient Egypt or the migration of geese. Why not give the legislator a copy? Viewing this CD-ROM could make for some interesting "computer time" after a hard day at the office or in a tense legislative session, and this will only emphasize the great works that you, as an educator, perform daily. Bringing the appropriate materials to a legislative office visit is a definite plus.

Now is the time to do your homework in preparation for the visit. You know the issues. You know what you want, and you know what you want the decision maker to do. If you will be discussing budgetary issues, be sure you know the appropriate facts and figures related to the current budget discussions. Be prepared to answer the tough questions that might arise. Be prepared with a couple of library stories that you or your colleagues can tell quickly that show how the kids in your community (the legislator's constituents) benefit from good school library programs. If you know specific facts about the legislator's own interests—golf, gardening, elephants—then you can figure out a way to include these in the conversation.

When the day of your appointment arrives, try to relax. Allow plenty of time to assure that you will arrive at the office promptly. Legislators and their staffs are very busy. There is something happening at every moment in their offices, and if you are late for an appointment, it not only speaks poorly of you, it also can cause a postponement that can delay your access to the legislator. Dress appropriately. You want to look professional, and you do not want to wear anything that would be distracting. But if you want to wear a particular T-shirt with a memorable library-related slogan that you have created, or a button stating your wishes/needs, that may be acceptable, depending upon the particular legislator, the formality of the office, the issues being discussed, and the people involved.

Keep topmost in your mind why you are there, what your priorities are, and the ultimate outcome that you expect as a result of your visit. In advance of the visit, talk with those who will accompany you about who will speak first and who will say what. It is customary for the person who made the arrangements for the visit to take the lead. Before you go in, be clear on the sequence in which each of you will speak.

Once you are escorted into the office, introductions are necessary. People in the delegation should introduce themselves and tell which school they represent or what other interest they have in the issue you came to discuss. Note: In many cases you will want to visit the legislator in whose district your school sits, even if you do not happen to live in that district. Remember that your students and their parents are constituents, so it is perfectly legitimate for you to advocate for them.

When you begin speaking about your issues try to speak in a conversational tone as much as possible. Remember techniques such as the "open face." Smile and be friendly. Be prepared to listen: legislators are very verbal people. Be polite, listen carefully, and if they say anything you can hook your information onto you might want to jot it down so you do not forget. This gives you the opportunity to say something like, "I'm glad you mentioned your use of the Internet. You might be interested in knowing that in the XYZ School library students are . . ." A statement such as this can lead you right into the real reasons why you are there. It is essential that you and your colleagues state your needs and desires in the clearest, briefest, most specific manner. Many of the techniques that apply to speaking before a board or a committee also apply on an office visit. The only differences are that your manner is more conversational and you may be interrupted to answer a question. Use your catchy sound bites to good advantage. Emphasize key points briefly, but more than once. If you are asked questions to which you do not know the answer, it is OK to say, "I don't know, but I can find that information and get back to you." The key here is to be sure you do get back to them in a timely fashion while they still remember the question they asked you. If you are asking the legislator to vote a certain way on a particular issue, it is also OK to say something like, "Can we count on your vote for school library materials funding?" Their answer to this question will be an indication of whether or not you have been successful, how committed they are to your requests, and whether there may be more work to be done. The main thing to remember on an office visit is to be positive, stay focused, have fun, and know when to stop! When the visit is over thank the legislator or staff person for her time. On the way out of the office, thank the scheduler and any other staff member you encounter.

After the visit, within a couple of days, write a thank-you note or letter. Thank them for taking the time to see you and reiterate briefly the purpose for your visit: *"Thank you so much for taking the time last Friday to discuss S123, the school library funding bill, with us."* There are many creative and interesting note cards on the market that show books or reading or that relate to libraries in some other way. Keep several of these around for use when you need them. You want your visit to be memorable, and you want to keep your name and your issues on the legislator's radar screen. A cute library-related thank-you card can often help to serve this purpose. It is also necessary to thank them after a vote has been cast. You can go to the Web sites that were mentioned in Chapter 2 (state and federal) and find out how votes were cast. If the legislator voted the way you wanted him to, a thank-you note or letter is in order. They need to know that their constituents are aware of what they are doing, and everyone responds positively to thanks. The reality is that you can never thank them too much!

After you have made your first visit to a legislator or board member's office, you will realize that it was not so difficult after all. Remember that they are just regular people who really want to do a good job. You will probably want to de-brief with your colleagues, so it is a good idea to organize a brief evaluation session that can provide help and ideas for your future endeavors. De-briefing and evaluating will give you an opportunity to determine the next steps, if any, and it will also allow you to decide if any changes need to be made the next time you are called upon to advocate for your school library program. When the next time rolls around, you will feel the empowerment of knowing exactly what you are doing since you will already know the people in the office. Future visits to legislative or school board offices will be easier!

Tips You Can Use Now

- **Be** very clear on what you want.

- **Bring** the appropriate people and materials.

- **Practice** the answers to possible "tough questions."

- **Be** bright; be brief; be gone.

- **Relax**, be friendly, have fun.

- **Thank**, thank, thank.

Telephone Calls

Sometimes in the midst of a legislative advocacy effort the time element can be so tight that telephone calls are the only effective way to contact decision makers. This is often true on the federal level. When the ALA Washington Office receives prior information of a particular legislative committee hearing or a House or Senate debate only a day or two before the actual event, members and senators must be contacted immediately. It is also often true on the state level, when the date of a vote on a particular bill is often not known until the day before, or even, amazingly, the very same morning.

All of the previous techniques for writing letters, speaking before boards and committees, and meeting in decision makers' offices also come into play when using the phone. Again, if you have a personal relationship with the staff members in the elected official's office, you will find a positive telephone encounter much easier to accomplish, since you will already know the name of the particular staff person to request, and your name will be known also. In legislative offices, the phones are ringing constantly, and the person who answers them (usually the receptionist that you probably met when you visited the local or capitol office) can become quite frazzled. This is when it is to your advantage to be able to say, "Hi Susie, this is John Jones from the X School Library Association. How are you? Is it possible for me to speak with George Williams for a few minutes about H1234, the school library bill that will be heard on the floor tomorrow?" If you do not know the name of a particular person for whom to ask, it usually works to ask for the staff member who is responsible for education issues.

Time is of the essence here. You will be able to tell by the tone of the person's voice that she is very busy. Staff members in legislative offices tend to be young, energetic men and women—often recently out of college—who are very sharp, very aware of political issues, very adept at multitasking, and always in a hurry. For these reasons you will need to state your desires very clearly and very quickly. If you are calling about a specific bill number, have that information in front of you. Nothing will turn these overachievers off more than someone on the other end of the phone who says something like, "Could you please vote for the library bill," and when asked the bill number does not know it. What works better is a statement like, *My name is Hank Johnson, I'm a constituent, and I'm calling to urge Congressman Lopez to vote in favor of H1234, the School Library Funding Bill.* If your district-wide or statewide advocacy network is working, the chances are that the office may have already received some similar calls, and the staff member with whom you speak will know exactly what you are talking about. It is not necessary for you to say more at this point, unless they ask you questions. They know what bills are up for a vote; they keep a running tally of phone calls from their constituents; and they share this information with the legislators throughout the day.

The key in using the phone for advocacy efforts is the same as with other methods: be bright, be brief, and be gone!

5

Library Legislative Days

Library Legislative Days have become a very effective advocacy tool on local, state, and national levels. They present an opportunity for a large group of librarians, library trustees and commissioners, friends, and other supporters to gather together in the state or national capitol for one purpose: to let their elected officials know their needs and wishes as related to their school, public, and university libraries. Library Legislative Days provide an opportunity for everyone to deliver the same message at the same time. They create a very strong impact on the decision makers who hold the purse strings.

In Washington, DC

In 1945 it became evident to the library community, specifically the ALA, that if libraries of all types were going to be adequately supported and funded by elected officials on the federal level it would be a good idea to have a strong presence in Washington, DC; thus, the ALA Washington Office was established. Located at 1300 Pennsylvania Avenue, just a few blocks from the White House, two separate ALA offices buzz with activity: the Office of Government Relations (OGR) and the Office for Information Technology Policy (OITP) which was established in 1995.

OGR "acts as a link between ALA members and the federal government, representing library interests and issues including: funding for federal library and related programs, telecommunications and postal rates, copyright, access to government information, the status of federal libraries and librarians, and other issues which affect the quality of library and information services to the American public" ("ALA Washington Office" n. pag.).

OITP "promotes the development and use of electronic access to information as a means to ensure the public's right to a free and open information society. Some major areas of interest for OITP include: equity of access, copyright, e-books, E-rate, and the information commons. OITP's primary activities include research and analysis, education, government representation, and strategic outlook activities" ("ALA Washington Office" n. pag.).

The role of the Washington Office is to act as a conduit in creating and maintaining links between the library community and the elected officials in Washington. They employ several lobbyists, each of whom is an expert in specific library-related issues, be they school library funding, copyright, intellectual freedom, or technology. The Washington Office lobbyists' clout comes from the fact that they represent library users, who are the best informed and articulate of all citizens, and who are constituents of every single one of the 100 senators and of the 435 members of congress. They are able to disseminate information to the grass roots advocates who are in every state, and they know where emphasis is needed during each step of the political process in which legislation is passed. These lobbyists also know the interests of each senator and member of congress, and can prepare grass roots advocates to plug their particular library stories into these varied interests when they are communicating with elected officials. Emily Sheketoff, Director of the ALA Washington Office, says, "I see my job as informing the grass roots so that they can put pressure on their elected officials" (Sheketoff n. pag.).

Another valued resource in Washington, DC is the National

Commission on Libraries and Information Science (NCLIS). The Commission was established by law on July 20, 1970, and its primary responsibility is to "advise the President and the Congress on the implementation of national policy [related to libraries] . . . conduct studies, surveys, and analysis of the library and information needs of the Nation . . . develop plans for meeting national library and information needs . . ." (The full charge of the Commission can be accessed at <www.nclis.gov/about.cfm>). The Commission includes the Librarian of Congress and fourteen members appointed by the President of the United States, of whom five are professional librarians or information specialists, and the remainder are citizens who have a particular competence or interest in our society's library needs and services. Commissioners serve for a term of five years.

NCLIS played a pivotal role in organizing both White House Conferences on Library and Information Services (1979 and 1991), and has held hearings throughout the United States on various library issues, including those specific to school libraries. In 2001 they held a hearing in Cincinnati, Ohio "to learn firsthand how the explosion of information technology has affected the work and status of school libraries and school librarians and how school libraries and school librarians are affecting student achievement" ("Hearings on School Libraries" n. pag.). The resulting report is in process, and when it is published, it will serve as an important resource for school librarians throughout the country, and it can be put to good use in all advocacy efforts. The key findings are listed in Appendix F. NCLIS was also instrumental in working with First Lady Laura Bush in organizing the White House Conference on School Libraries in Washington, DC in June, 2002.

The ALA Washington Office organized the first National Library Legislative Day in 1974. Today it is co-sponsored by the District of Columbia Library Association, and is usually held on the first Tuesday in May. Legislative Day brings librarians, library trustees, board members, and other library friends to Washington, DC to speak personally with U.S. senators or representatives or their staff members. There are usually from 300-500 participants, and each year nearly all 50 states are represented. Legislative Day provides an opportunity for librarians from all types of libraries to communicate with each other regarding the similarities and differences in their issues. It also provides an opportunity for them to support each other's requests where elected officials are concerned.

National Library Legislative Day has now grown to a two-day event. On Monday there is an all-day briefing session. After welcome messages from the hosts and announcements, there are in-depth briefings on all of the issues that will be discussed with legislators on Tuesday, and an opportunity for participants to ask questions. Often there are breakout groups where specific issues such as ESEA, the Library Services and Technology Act (LSTA), Copyright, E-Rate, etc. are discussed in greater depth. Each attendee receives a packet filled with the Issues Briefs—each a one-pager printed on a different color paper that bullets the important points to be made related to that issue. Packets are provided for each legislator as well.

A state coordinator is appointed by each state library agency to lead that state's delegation in Washington. The library supporters from the particular state have already made appointments in advance with all of the congressional representatives and the two U.S. Senators from that state, and a schedule is created showing which people are to visit which offices. The state coordinator picks up the packets for that state's legislators and distributes them to the library advocates who will be visiting their offices. For a small state such as Rhode Island or a large state with a small population such as Wyoming, participants will only have to visit a few offices, and the whole delegation may visit all of the offices together. But for a state like California, with 53 members of Congress to visit, quite a hectic day awaits—especially if there are a small number of Legislative Day participants. For this reason, the larger state delegations often schedule some of their appointments on Monday instead of Tuesday.

On Tuesday, the whole day, until about 4:00 p.m., is devoted to visiting the congressional and senatorial offices. Depending upon the size of your delegation to Washington, you will probably have one or more Legislative Day participants accompanying you. Usually the state coordinators divide their delegations, especially larger ones, into teams of two or maybe three people. You will probably be paired with a public librarian, someone from your State Library, or a library trustee, friend, or other supporter. While you are walking to your appointments you can decide who will say what and who will emphasize what points when the meeting actually begins. You can also decide on the sequence in which each of you will speak.

Wear comfortable shoes! The congressional offices are located in three buildings on Capitol Hill—which really *is* a hill!—the Cannon House Office Building (CHOB), the Rayburn House Office Building (RHOB), and the Longworth House Office Building (LHOB). If your state has a large congressional delegation, there is a big possibility, no matter how you try to avoid it, that you will be trudging up and down the hill from building to building, and the weather in Washington in May can be anything from hot to rainy to (sometimes) wonderful! Your trudging can be eased a bit, especially if the weather is not great, by underground tunnels that connect the buildings. If you use these, you will walk through long, dull-looking hallways, but you will avoid getting wet or suffering from heat prostration, and at least they are flat.

Once you enter the particular congressional office building, you will need to go through security—all bags, etc. on a conveyor belt, and a walk through a metal detector—just like at the airport. These buildings were built quite a long time ago, and there are all sorts of interesting statues, plaques, and other things of historical interest to view. Their floor plans are quite interesting also, and, in some cases, not unlike a maze. However, they do have relatively good signage and maps, and it usually is not too difficult to find the office you are seeking. It is quite thrilling to walk through the halls. You may see media people gathered with their microphones and video cameras outside of one particular office, which usually means that particular member of congress is embroiled in some important or controversial piece of legislation, and will probably have a statement on the evening news. You might even see an interview in process right there in the hallway! You really get the feeling that important business is going on here, and you realize that all of these men and women in Congress have been elected by their constituents to come to Washington to work for *them*. In front of each congress member's office is a large flag from the member's state. The flags are especially helpful if you are at the end of one of the long hallways—you can just look down the hall for your particular state flag, and that helps you locate the office easily. The names of the members and their states, along with the room numbers, are emblazoned in gold letters on the lush-looking oak doors.

Once you enter the member's office, look around. It is very interesting to note how they have decorated their reception areas. Many have artwork done by children, beautiful photos of points of interest in their states, awards or commemorative plaques, maps of their districts, or interesting pieces of art. Some of the offices are large and beautiful, with amazing views of the Capitol building across the street. Others seem to be quite tiny. A lot depends on seniority and committee membership. You will notice that a television is constantly on in the reception area. It is either tuned to the session on the floor of the House, if a session is scheduled, or to CNN. On one afternoon in Washington a couple of years ago, CNN was showing a car chase in Los Angeles. This was especially amusing to this Los Angeles, California writer nearly 3,000 miles from home!

Introduce yourself to the receptionist, and provide her with your business card, if you have one, and let those accompanying you do the same. If you are fortunate enough to meet personally with the congress member, you will be ushered into their private office. This might happen immediately, or you might have to wait. They may be in the middle of another meeting that has gone overtime, or they may be on their way back from a vote in the House. In the inner office you will also see more plaques and awards, often pictures of them with the current or a past President of the United States, and more beautiful art. If you are meeting with a staff person, you may meet in the member's office if the House is in session, in a small conference room—if there is one, or maybe just sitting on a couch in the reception area. Sometimes they will invite you down to a lounge or coffee area in another part of the building, and your meeting will continue there, and sometimes you will even meet with them just standing in the hallway outside the office!

When you are actually discussing the issues you came to discuss, all of the same rules and suggestions apply that were put forth in Chapter 4. Remember that time is of the essence and you need to be clear, concise, and quick! Leave the packet containing the "Issues Briefs" that was provided for you on Monday. You might want to point out specific pages to bring particular matters to the congress member's or staff's attention. If you have business cards, be sure to leave one, along with an offer to provide additional information should they need it. When you are ready to leave, thank them for their time, and do not forget to also thank the staff people in the outer office. Be sure to pick up a business card for each legislator or staff person with whom you have met. You will need these when you write your thank-you notes or letters after returning home.

Lunch on Capitol Hill is fun. Each of the buildings has a cafeteria/lunch room for its employees, and the cafeteria is also open to the public. The lunchroom in the Longworth Building is similar to a food court at the mall! There are all kinds of choices, from deli to pizza to Chinese to salad bar, and a large variety of cold drinks in large refrigerated cases. There is always a feeling of excitement in the Longworth cafeteria, because you never know who will be eating there on any given day. Most of the congressional staff members eat there (when they take time to eat!) and you will often see some of the members of Congress themselves. You will also invariably see large groups of students of all ages on school tours—often wearing their school shirts or uniforms. They, of course, are acting like kids do everywhere! You will think you are in your school cafeteria, and you will have to stifle the urge to act like a typical teacher who wants to remind them to throw away their trash or stop yelling. There is also a House of Representatives gift shop next to the cafeteria, where you can purchase all sorts of neat souvenirs with the House logo—anything from key rings, pencils, or refrigerator magnets to T-shirts and scarves or gorgeous bronze bookends or crystal paperweights. There are also books and items for children.

If you are lucky, the schedule for your visits will have been made so that the congressional appointments are all in the morning, and the senatorial appointments in the afternoon, or vice versa. The Senate office buildings are all the way across the Capitol Complex on the opposite side of those for the House. Again, this is a substantial walk, but if the weather is pleasant you can enjoy the sights. At one time you could ride a tram from the House side to the Senate side of Capitol Hill, but due to security measures put in place after September 11, 2001, it is now only available for members and senators. As you walk across the Capitol Complex, you will pass by the impressive Library of Congress and the Supreme Court on your right, and the U.S. Capitol building on your left.

The senatorial offices are also in three buildings: the Russell Senate Office Building (RSOB), the Dirksen Senate Office Building (DSOB), and the Hart Senate Office Building (HSOB). Your visits to the senate offices will be similar to those in the congressional buildings. You will go through security, and once in the senators' offices you will follow the same procedures and use the same techniques. Again, be sure to thank everyone and to pick up business cards as you leave each office.

At this point, you are probably dead tired, but your day is not over yet! Usually, early on Tuesday evening, after all of the legislative office visits have been completed, the ALA Washington Office hosts a reception in one of the congressional office buildings. There will be welcome refreshments, and you will have the opportunity to mingle with library supporters from all over the country. You will also meet school librarians from other states with whom you can chat and share stories about your library program or compare notes about your legislative office visits. The ALA Washington Office often presents awards at this reception to legislators who have been especially strong library supporters, and since you are right there in the same room you can take the opportunity to meet them, shake their hand, and thank them for their support. You might also have a chance to meet other senators or members of congress at the reception, since they are all invited, and there are always some who do attend. In 2003 consumer advocate Ralph Nader was in attendance, as was Rep. Bernie Sanders (I-VT), who wrote important legislation insuring privacy to library users, and received an ALA award.

Whether you arrived in the nation's capitol by plane, train, bus, or car, on the way home you can reflect on the National Library Legislative Day experience and feel a great sense of accomplishment since you will know you have played an important part in influencing the decision makers of our nation. You are one of a select few concerned citizens who has taken the time to fight for something you strongly believe in: your school library.

In Your State Capitol

A large number of states organize annual Library Legislative Days in their state capitols. These Legislative Days take different forms in different states, and are usually coordinated by the state library association, often in conjunction with the state school library association, friends of libraries groups, or library trustees and commissioners. If you do not already know whether your state even has a Library Legislative Day, you can probably find this information by contacting the state library association or even your state library agency. The major purpose of a statewide Library Legislative Day is to bring the accomplishments of the different types of libraries and the concerns of the library community to the attention of state elected officials and the Governor. It is also an excellent occasion for attendees to learn effective legislative advocacy techniques, to show that a large number of state residents support their state's school, public, and academic libraries and realize their value to people of all ages, and to thank legislators for their past support. Often there is specific legislation that is being heard, either by a committee or by one or more of the state legislative bodies. Legislative Day is a perfect opportunity to urge state legislators to support legislation related to state funding for school, public, and academic libraries.

If you have not visited your state capitol, this is a terrific opportunity to do so. You will be able to see firsthand how the political process works in your state and what a difference positive advocacy makes. It can almost be considered a staff development activity in learning how the government works.

Since the experience of this writer comes from being involved in statewide Library Legislative Days in Sacramento, California, the following is a picture of California's development of school library participation in Legislative Days both in the state capitol and in the local district office as possible models for others to follow.

The California Library Association (CLA) has been organizing an annual Library Legislative Day in the state capital in Sacramento since 1982, when it became evident that it was essential for librarians, library friends and trustees, and library users to communicate with California's assemblymembers and state senators in order to achieve optimum funding support for California's libraries of all types. Legislative Day has traditionally been held each year on a Tuesday in late April or early May. The involvement throughout the early years of school library people in Legislative Day was quite minimal. The various historical incarnations of the California School Library Association (CSLA) had been working for years to garner state support for school libraries, with results that were largely unimpressive. In 1992 the tide began to change when the association's board of directors voted to hire a new lobbyist—one whose specialty was education issues—and one who had a belief in the necessity for state K-12 library support.

In 1993, following the advice of the association's lobbyist, the CSLA Board of Directors voted to co-sponsor Library Legislative Day along with CLA, and a few years later Friends of California Libraries (FCL) joined in the co-sponsorship. The synergy of these three groups of library supporters has been very positive for all concerned. For school librarians it has provided an arena in which to educate the other members of the California library community on school library issues, and to solicit their support when specific legislation for school libraries has been introduced in the California legislature. By the same token, school library people are able to advocate for public and academic library issues when they are called upon to do so. On Legislative Day, delegations to individual state legislators' offices are comprised of members from all three co-sponsoring groups as well as members of the California Association of Library Trustees and Advocates (CALTAC), who approach with a united front for California's libraries, even though each may be asking the legislators for a vote on a different library-related issue.

Planning for Library Legislative Day usually begins by asking library supporters to mark the specific dates for Legislative Day in their calendars since the dates are generally known well in advance. Planning ahead gives people a chance not only to mark their calendars, but also to begin thinking about saving money for the excursion, since most school library participants attend this activity at their own expense. Because of the size of California, it is necessary for many attendees to plan on air travel and a night in a hotel. The same would probably be true in states like Texas or Florida. This is quite different from a state such as Rhode Island where a colleague once said, "We can call a meeting in the capitol and no one has to drive more than 45 minutes to get there." This obviously is not the case in California!

In March, CSLA sends out a "LegiLetter" to its entire membership, which provides the details for participation in the upcoming Legislative Day. It includes a bulleted list of the pertinent issues that will be discussed, the message we need to impart, the agenda for the day, information on hotels and air travel, and a registration form. This information is also provided on our school library listserv, CALIBK12. In recent years, it has been possible to register electronically as well on the CLA or CSLA Web sites. Registration is available to association members, and the fee is reasonable: usually $20 or $25; nonmembers may participate also at a fee that is slightly higher. On site registration is available also, again at a slightly higher fee than advance registration.

Meanwhile, our lobbyist begins preparing the school library-related "Issues Brief" that will be placed in the packets that will be provided for each attendee and each state legislator. CLA coordinates the creation of the packets in their Sacramento office, and the actual stuffing is done the weekend before Legislative Day with help from people from both associations.

CSLA and CLA maintain a database of legislative contacts. These are people, many of whom are school librarians, who have each agreed to be the contact person for a specific state assemblymember or senator— usually the one who either represents the district where they live or the one in which they work. A "legislative contact coordinator" informs the contacts via an e-mail list when they need to begin making the appointments, and as appointments are confirmed all of the information is maintained in the database. When it gets closer to the actual day, the contact coordinator is able to create a list of all of the appointments, which can be printed out, and individuals can find out who else will be joining them on a particular appointment. This information is also available on Legislative Day itself.

In 2001, the CSLA Governmental Relations Committee decided that it would be a good idea if school librarians coming to Sacramento for Legislative Day could meet together beforehand to clarify their issues and ask any questions, so a school library caucus is now scheduled for the Monday evening before Legislative Day. Since most of the people who need to travel long distances arrive in Sacramento on Monday evening anyway, participants' attendance at the caucus has been excellent. At the Caucus the lobbyist can provide up-to-the-minute information on specific bills that are being heard in the legislature, and can let school library supporters know which points they need to emphasize in their office visits on the following day.

Library Legislative Day itself, on Tuesday, is very similar to National Library Legislative Day in Washington, DC (see previous section). CSLA members assist the CLA staff at the registration tables, and there is time to enjoy morning refreshments, network with colleagues, and pick up packets. The legislative contacts pick up the packets that will be given to the legislators. There is a morning briefing, the CSLA and CLA lobbyists explain the issues, and participants begin making their office visits. In the late afternoon all may reconvene for a de-briefing session, where participants can share the results of their office visits: which legislators were positive, questions that may have been asked, or which legislators need more education related to school library issues. Sometimes attendees may be asked to fill out feedback forms where they can list important outcomes from the meetings they have had. This varies from year to year. If feedback forms are used, they are dropped in a box that is provided at a central point, and they are then given to the lobbyists for CSLA and CLA, who can use this information as they continue their daily work of monitoring the legislation, making statements before committees or on the floor of the legislature when necessary, and keeping the memberships of all four organizations informed on the progress of specific bills.

California school librarians who have participated in Library Legislative Day for the first time are usually hooked! They have made statements like, "I was explaining my library program to Senator X and he really listened to me. I felt so empowered!" or, "There was a library trustee in our group who is planning to go home and explore the situation in the school libraries in his neighborhood, and we are going to work together and organize some meetings with parents." We have been able to generate many more school library supporters among library trustees and friends group members simply as a result of the acquaintances that were initially made on Legislative Day. Another positive outcome is that first-time participants are so excited about this event that they decide to bring a colleague the following year, or perhaps parents or students, and attendance by school library supporters has increased from 37 in 1993 to more than 100 in 2003.

One of the best outcomes of school librarians' participation in Library Legislative Days was the passage of the California Public School Library Act of 1998, which, for the first time in the history of the state, provided a separate and specific line item in the state budget exclusively for the funding of school library materials and technology. The actual funding in this line item provided $28 per student in every public school in California. The $28 figure remained in effect for four years, and this enormous influx of state money allowed school librarians to weed their collections and to begin to bring California's books-per-student average out of the dungeon. Even though it suffered an enormous cut in 2003, the line item remained, due entirely to grass roots advocacy that strengthened state legislators' awareness of the importance of school libraries to the total instructional program in every K-12 school in California.

Statewide Library Legislative Days are an excellent vehicle for telling the school library story, for sharing the research showing the connection between strong school library programs and raised student achievement, and for creating a groundswell of support for school library funding that legislators cannot ignore.

In the Local District

As successful as school library people in California have been with Legislative Day in Sacramento, the harsh reality is that it is often very difficult for school librarians to leave their duties at school and travel to Sacramento—albeit for an excellent purpose that can only benefit the school. For others, the expense just does not fit into their personal budgets. Also, in many school districts, if the librarian is absent, no substitute is provided, which often means that the library has to be closed.

It is somewhat ironic to be in the capitol lobbying for your library, while back at home students and teachers are unable to have access to the materials they need since the library is closed. For these reasons, CSLA and CLA decided to organize "Legislative Day in the District" in 2002.

The chosen day was a Friday in early February. Friday was selected since legislators leave Sacramento on Thursday evening and generally spend Friday in their local district offices. February was chosen because it falls near the beginning of the California legislative session, and the rationale was that any library-related bills would have already been introduced, or would be soon. If there was no specific piece of legislation that needed action, the day could be used as a meet-and-greet education session—an opportunity to meet the legislators and their staff members at home, where they are often more relaxed and less pressed for time. It would also provide school librarians with an opportunity to include parents, teachers, and students, to bring examples of students' projects, and to present themselves as the local "school library experts." Although many public library supporters have also participated in Day in the District, the vast majority has consisted, since its inception, of school library advocates.

The legislative contact coordinator again informs the legislative contacts when they need to begin making the appointments in the local district offices. Since the district offices are generally not too far away, school librarians can request that the appointments be made late on Friday afternoon so that they do not need to spend any time away from school. In some of the less densely populated rural areas of California, the state legislators' offices might require a long drive, but even if a school librarian must leave school an hour or two earlier than usual—especially on a Friday—at least they do not have to miss the entire day. Information on confirmed appointments is again gathered in a database, and participants are informed through CALIBK12 (school) and CALIX (public), the two statewide library listservs, on how to access their own appointments as well as to indicate whether they will attend. As the Day in the District nears, each legislative contact can print out a list of those who will attend the meeting in the district office. The listservs also refer people to the CSLA and CLA Web sites, where they can access and print out the necessary "Issues Briefs" or other documents that provide the details or bulleted points for their discussions in the local offices or those that are designed specifically to be presented to the legislators.

The success of California's Library Legislative Day in the District has been phenomenal! Participants have been thrilled with the wonderful conversations they have had with their state legislators. In many cases they were able to spend as long as 30-45 minutes in the local office, which gave them a chance to explain their library programs in greater detail, and to provide information on the critical role that the school librarian plays in the total instructional process. Legislators agreed to continue their support of school libraries, and even during a very dire budget crisis in California in 2003, many of them made a commitment to maintain California's school library materials line item in the state budget, even though it would have to take a huge cut. Given that there were some moves afoot to eliminate this line altogether at the beginning of the year, this was a great victory for California's K-12 libraries.

Participation in Library Legislative Days in the local district, in the state capitol, or in Washington, DC is a very potent method of bringing the library story to elected officials. Amazing gains have been made throughout the country by libraries of all types as a result of contacts made on Library Legislative Days. Participants tend to return again and again, knowing that their voice truly counts.

Tips You Can Use Now

- **Consult** your state library or state library association to determine whether annual Library Legislative Days are scheduled in your state capitol.

- **Start** now to contact your school library colleagues about attending. Provide information regarding dates, cost, etc. so that they can begin planning ahead.

- **If** your school library association is not involved in a Legislative Day, suggest to the leadership that they might want to begin to consider it. Suggest cooperation between the school and public library associations, if that is applicable. Explore the possibility of having a Legislative Day in the District. Select a colleague who is computer-savvy to design a database of your association's membership that can be connected with legislators' names and individual appointment times. (For answers to questions on how the database is created and used, contact John McGinnis, Director of the Library at Cerritos College in California at *mcginnis@cerritos.edu*.)

- **Include** the participation of parents, teachers, students, and other community members.

- **Always** remember to write thank-you notes or letters after the event has concluded.

6

Success Stories

School library advocates throughout the United States have had successful advocacy projects and experiences in the various activities that have been organized in their school districts or their states. Whether they were appearances before boards of education, legislative days, statewide events, or connections with their teachers' unions, the results were greater support for school libraries. Following are a few of their stories.

An Almost Perfect Scenario

Recently in Kansas City, Missouri, 24 school librarians' positions, over one-third of the school district's 69, were threatened with elimination due to a large budget deficit. Kansas City librarians took matters into their own hands, and their story, a day-by-day chronology, is presented here. Although the names and the specific dates have been omitted to protect the privacy of the people involved, the story must be told, so imagine, as pioneer radio journalist Edward R. Murrow used to say, "You are there."

Day One: The superintendent holds an open forum at one of the Kansas City high schools to share the 2003-2004 Kansas City, Missouri School District (KCMSD) budget proposal with the public. This budget would be presented to the school board for a vote on June 25. He announces that budget cuts include 24 librarian positions, approximately one-third of the district's librarians. The Kansas City Federation of Teachers (KCFT) president is alarmed by the proposal to cut librarians, as it had not been an issue in any previous budget talks.

Day Two: The KCFT president advises the district library services director and a school librarian of the proposed cuts and that the budget will be presented to the board the next evening. How do you fight something so big in less than 24 hours? First, the librarian who receives the information contacts others. The KCFT president then advises us to attend the board meeting, but she has little hope we can stop the train. Someone calls a board member to express concern over such a sudden drastic cut. He says he will do what he can.

Day Three: The library services director, KCFT president, and three librarians watch the school board vote 6-2 in favor of the budget, including the slashing of the 24 librarians, with no discussion of the issue. One of the dissenting board members stands up to decry the ill-advised cut of essential personnel. The KCFT president advises us that our only hope is to get on the agenda of the district's Finance and Audit Committee to plead our case. We will have to convince them to recommend an amendment to the budget that would reinstate the 24 librarians' positions. That night, three of us, on the advice of our director and union president, plan a meeting of all of the district's librarians. We divide the list among us so that every librarian receives a personal phone call about the school board's vote and about the meeting planned for the 30th of June.

Days Four Through Seven: The alarm is sounded and the battle begins. An article appears in the *Kansas City Star* announcing the passage of the budget, which cut one-third of us. According to minimum state standards, a school with less than 600 students would not have a full-time librarian. That would mean only a handful of our elementary schools would retain a full-time librarian. The phone tree begins and librarians begin to make noise—telling principals, teachers, neighbors, anyone who will listen—that this cut is disastrous. The meeting is planned for the afternoon of Monday, June 30th at a local public library. We begin to make a list of reasons why we are essential partners in the education of our students.

Day Eight: More than 50 of our 70+ librarians come together to organize a campaign to do what appears to be an impossible task: asking the school board to go against the superintendent's recommendation. Our director reminds us that just a few years ago, the school board made a good faith statement that every school would have a full-time librarian, even though it was not a state mandate. Our district will be evaluated for full accreditation by the state next year. In our favor, the state requires that every library in every school be staffed before and after school and during the school day. If those of us who are left become traveling librarians, who will staff the libraries when we are not there? Our union president promises to help in any way she can, including getting us on the agenda of the Finance and Audit Committee, calling board members, and sending out a press release. Librarians leave the meeting with hope, strength, and determination. We will not go quietly!

Days Nine Through Fifteen: Faced with a holiday weekend when many are out of town, we begin to network. We truly experience the power of organizing, strategizing, and networking. We notify teachers, principals, parents, neighbors, the press, Laura Bush, Oprah Winfrey, anyone who will listen to our story about the repercussions of the board's impulsive decision to slash and burn our library program. We, along with the hundreds of supporters, flood the e-mail boxes of the school board members, burn the telephone wires leaving voice mail messages asking to be heard, write letters to the board and to the local newspaper. We make a lot of noise and a lot of sense.

Day Sixteen: The morning edition of the *Kansas City Star* runs an article about our struggle. It is positive and informative and seems to support us. We appear at the KCMSD offices for the Finance and Audit Committee meeting. We are 50 or more, all wearing buttons saying, "Libraries are the heart of the school!" made by one of our colleagues. We have librarians, parents, and teachers there in support of our cause. The committee has to move the meeting from a small conference room to the large auditorium to accommodate our crowd. The committee is composed of four board members, but seven of the nine are in attendance. This is our first indication that we have been heard!

The meeting is called to order. We are first on the agenda. Our KCFT president speaks on our behalf. She makes the plea with facts, figures, and research-based conclusions. She is convincing and we begin to see board members sit a little straighter, lean forward, and watch the superintendent look a bit worried. He speaks against us, reminding board members that the budget is tight and something must go, but we say, "Not us! We are in the schools doing the work and helping kids." One of our colleagues has written a letter to board members about just that— what we do in a day, a week, a school year. Her letter is read aloud and it touches all of us with the emotion of what will be lost. Board members begin to ask questions about who will be in the libraries when we are not, and how will this affect our accreditation? We hear board members reminding each other and the superintendent that the school board must keep children in mind, that cuts in the budget should be carefully researched and questioned, that impulsive slashing is just that. It is amazing to watch the tide turn, to hear the school board president say that he is inclined to believe we are necessary and important and that they must find the money to keep every library staffed.

Under a banner in the auditorium that reads, "Is it good for the children?" the committee votes unanimously to recommend that the budget be amended to reinstate the 24 library positions. We exhale.

Day Eighteen: We arrive at the board meeting with our buttons and with hope. It is anticlimactic at best. In a simple vote, the recommendation is made and the board unanimously votes "Yes." In our confusion, we slowly slip outside and realize that we have won! We did it! We made a difference! We congratulate each other and realize that it is not over yet, for next year the ax will rear its ugly head again. But for now, we celebrate and return to our schools with renewed spirit and energy (Anonymous n. pag.).

The point of this wonderful story from Kansas City is the passion, the collaboration, the reliance on facts and research, and the emphasis on benefits to students. In a nutshell it presents a picture of what this book is about.

Although the political situation, the players, the issues, and the reality in each school district and each state are quite different, two facts remain:

1. Political advocacy is often needed.
2. When you do it, it works.

Anyone can learn to become a political advocate; and, like with any other new skill, the more you do it, the easier it becomes. You can start at the simplest level: knowing the facts and presenting them to your own school's faculty and principal. From there you can move on to making presentations to district level administrators or to school boards. Once you have mastered these skills and decided, "I can do this," you can graduate to serious political advocacy on state and national levels.

One thing that is evident in the Kansas City story is the amount of support and advice provided by the union president. It is becoming more and more apparent to those of us who have spent many years in the school library world that this type of connection is a boat that we have been missing. It stands to reason: in one school there is one librarian—perhaps more in those schools that are exceptionally fortunate—but there are many teachers. In a large urban middle or high school there could be 100-150 teachers. The school community includes a myriad number of parents, business people, and others who would be natural supporters of school libraries if only they were asked. The old fable, "A Bundle of Sticks" had a moral: In unity there is strength. And another old saying tells us, "There is strength in numbers." What worked in Kansas City was a large, unified group of librarians and their strongest allies—the teachers, parents, neighbors, and others who were galvanized by school library leaders to take a stand.

School Library Staffing Negotiated

Doug Johnson, the director of media and technology in the Mankato, Minnesota public school district and the current president of the Minnesota Educational Media Organization (MEMO) put it this way:

"Another avenue that I am not sure has been thoroughly explored (at least here in Minnesota) is the influence that media specialists can have in their teacher organizations. Education Minnesota is a powerful influence in the state on funding, certification issues, standards, etc. and most media specialists belong to it since they are certified teachers and their substantial dues fund lobbyists and political actions . . . Do school library media specialists need to get more active in this area?" (Johnson, "Budget Cuts" n. pag.)

What Doug states above is true in most states. The teachers' associations present a most powerful lobby in every state capitol. They represent the teachers who teach the hundreds of thousands or even millions of children and young people throughout the state. There are few people anywhere who do not want the best for children. Period. Becoming involved in the teachers' associations might just be the current best answer in proactive advocacy for school libraries.

Roz Sudakow, the librarian at Woodbridge High School in Irvine, California says, "Involvement is the key." She currently serves as the secretary of the Irvine Teachers' Association (ITA), which enables her to sit on the board and constantly provide information regarding school library issues. She knows that librarians' presence on the governing body of the local union is absolutely essential, and that this is the only way to keep library issues continuously in the conversation.

Roz began her activism by becoming the ITA representative from her school, and she feels that this is the important first step that school librarians must take to begin to place their message into the culture of the local. "If you don't say anything, it's going to be forgotten," she says (Sudakow n. pag.). The previous librarian at Woodbridge High, now retired, was Gail Rothman, who served for four years as the president of ITA in the 1990s and was a passionate advocate for school libraries. She had been very active on ITA's board for years, and served on the bargaining committee even before being elected president. She was instrumental in obtaining the inclusion of mandatory credentialed librarians in the middle and high schools in the Irvine Unified School District's contract. Prior to that it was left to each school to decide whether they would have a librarian or not.

Roz presents the following five major points for becoming proactive with your local union:

- "Become a school building representative in your local. Don't be afraid to get involved. Work up through the ranks to a leadership position so that you can sit on the board where decisions are made. If you have the opportunity to run for a state-level association office, do it; or become a representative from your local to the state association's governing council.
- Assure that the members of the local understand that you are a teacher, who, along with the classroom teacher, is part of a collaborative instructional team at the school. Do not allow them to ever forget this fact, and the part that you, the librarian, play in the education of students.
- Provide information concerning school libraries to the leadership of the local at every opportunity. When legislative issues arise that need action, be they on the school district or the state level, enlist the cooperation of the local and its members in your advocacy efforts.
- Write articles for your local association's regular newsletter or other

communication that is sent to all members. Present the issues that affect the libraries in your district, and show how these issues also affect teachers and students. Keep librarians constantly on their minds.

• Recruit younger librarians in your district to become active in the local teachers' association. The strong "fighters" eventually retire, and there needs to be someone with new energy to carry the ball. Bring a young colleague along to a meeting to allay any fears she may have about becoming involved" (Sudakow n. pag.).

Roz knows that her local teachers' union has power, and by inserting school library issues into the union's culture and mindset she also creates power for librarians.

Another Voice for Union Involvement—At the State Level

Marie-Anne Harkness, librarian at Camelot Elementary School in the Federal Way Public School District in Auburn, Washington and the Immediate Past-President of the Washington Library Media Association (WLMA), is another strong supporter of school librarians' involvement in their teachers' unions. She has a history of participating in activities with her political party, and realized some years ago that she also needed to be involved in other arenas in order to accomplish necessary goals. She works closely with Jennifer Maydole, the legislative liaison for WLMA, and has created a strong relationship between WLMA and the Washington Education Association (WEA).

This partnership with WEA has resulted in the WLMA/WEA formation of a joint committee, of which Marie-Anne is now the chair, which works toward furthering the clout of librarians in their state and local teachers' associations. The joint committee is made up of WLMA members and the WEA staff member in charge of Libraries and Academic Freedom. The joint committee has published prototype bargaining language (see Appendix E), and a WEA lobbyist assigned to the State Board of Education and the Office of the Superintendent of Public Instruction has lobbied on WLMA's behalf with the state board. Plans are in preparation for supporting the development of marketing strategies on building, district, region, and state levels.

In her own school district Marie-Anne has developed a strong relationship with the head of the Federal Way Public School District bargaining team, Monica Strictland, who has done excellent work in supporting the professionalism of school librarians in the district's contract language. Marie-Anne provides the following rationale and guidelines:

"It is critical to our political well-being to cooperate and collaborate with political organizations that have the power to affect school library media programs. Groups that have enormous impact are the local and state education associations affiliated with the National Education Association (NEA) and the American Federation of Teachers (AFT). These groups represent all school-certificated staff but because of sheer numbers, represent the interests of the classroom teacher above all else. However, most state organizations recognize the needs of the specialist groups and will provide some support if approached assertively.

The assertive approach is based on grass roots involvement. If every building had one school librarian representative, the effect would make a strong statement. If every representative body had one school librarian on the governing board or executive committee, the effect would be powerful. If every school district had one school librarian representative to the state representative body, that would be enormous. But most powerful of all would be if every district had one school librarian on the bargaining team.

At the bargaining table is where the power exists to either weaken or strengthen the role of the school librarian. Last minute deals can destroy collaboration, the heart of the instructional role. Assertive involvement at all levels of the association can work to diminish these 'deals'—such as work day planning time, playground and bus duty, instructional materials for the classroom vs. funding for library instructional materials, and many more.

Just like working the political process in the republican and democratic parties, start small and work upward by communicating with the 'powers that be.' Real change happens from within, so become an active member of your education association. Find out the issues at your building and become a leader by representing the building at the monthly representative body meeting. Most buildings have more than one representative and are still underrepresented, so this is a great place to start. Become a team player with your building's representatives and speak up for your building's causes at the assembly. Becoming an active building rep is a foot in the door.

Learn more about your state teachers' organization and set up opportunities to network with other school districts by running for your association's representative to the state representative assembly. As you learn more about your state organization, inquire about the people running for state association office. If someone is interested in school library programs, work for that person's campaign. This is like being invited to come in.

Run for office after a year or two of being a building representative. Start with a representative-at-large or similar position, or better yet: be a political action representative. The secretary or treasurer is another powerful hero of the executive committee. At executive committee meetings opportunities will become available to you to attend leadership-training sessions provided by the state organization. Attend these leadership-training sessions and especially learn about bargaining. To serve on the executive committee is like being invited to sit at the table.

Get to know your state organization's staff and leadership. Communicate directly when you can sincerely compliment someone for a job well done. Speak to the person at the state level who works directly with your state school library association, or whose purview includes school library programs. This person is your advocate and valued partner who can help you advocate with your state government and board of education. Finding and developing a positive relationship with your state level staff person is like being asked to help with the dishes. (Female bonding, come on!)

Write letters to the editor of your state teachers' association's journal or newsletter. Participate in a work group or committee. Be a visible school library supporter. Talk up your successes and voice problems that you want solved in a creative and optimistic matter. Be respectful and assertive. With hard work and smart networking you will get positive results" (Harkness n. pag.).

Starting Small—Recruiting Allies

One of the keys to becoming a successful school library advocate is to begin right in your very own school. You know the culture and the players, and you can establish positive relationships with your principal, your teachers, and the parents. This is exactly what happened in Unionville Elementary School in Monroe, North Carolina.

Debbie Hargett is the elementary school library media coordinator in the Union County Public Schools. Her principal asked that she work with kindergarten and fifth grade teachers at Unionville Elementary to create presentations for parents during kindergarten orientation and fifth grade graduation. She went a step further and created a PowerPoint presentation, which featured the Parent-Teacher Organization (PTO) and all of the things they do for teacher appreciation. Her presentation introduced the parents and the site-based governing committee that makes the financial decisions for the school to the great potential for technology, and what it could do for students. With a few key people seeing this "value added" that a school librarian brings to the educational process Debbie feels that committee members will be receptive to future proposals.

Because of a lesson plan proposal that Debbie wrote, which highlighted how technology would be incorporated into the classroom, Union County recently awarded the Unionville elementary school library more than $3000 in cutting edge technology. Now that the equipment has been received, the lesson plan is a reality, and the kids win (Hargett n. pag.).

This is the type of proactive advocacy at the school level that can lead to bigger and better things! If a situation arises in Unionville where librarians' jobs are threatened or there is a chance for additional funding for materials or technology, it is most likely that Debbie can call on the parents and teachers to join in advocacy efforts at the school district or state level. She has already created allies who understand the role that the school librarian plays in the education of children. They can present a unified front whenever and wherever their efforts are needed.

Working with the State Department of Education and the State Library

Many state school library associations are not in a position to employ lobbyists. In these cases, much of the advocacy efforts are indirectly done through becoming involved in and supporting the efforts of the State Department of Education or the State Library Agency.

Deb Logan is the librarian at Mt. Gilead High School in Mt. Gilead, Ohio and the Advocacy Chair for the Ohio Educational Library Media Association (OELMA). She has worked with the leaders of OELMA to encourage school librarians to become involved in the writing teams that created the state-mandated *Content Standards for Ohio Schools* in all of the academic curricular areas. Ohio's Content Standards include information literacy, technology literacy, and media literacy in all curricular areas. The strongest manifestation of this is a research strand in the Language Arts and Social Studies Standards, and the presence of information skills in Science and Math. Becoming involved in writing Content Standards and integrating information skills is one of the ways that school librarians in Ohio have responded to the school library cuts in Ohio's Operating Standards, which were legislated in December, 2000 and became a reality in the fall of 2001.

The presence of a state school library coordinator in the Department of Education was a great help in OELMA's efforts. She was able to provide a voice for school libraries throughout the department, raising awareness of the essential role of school libraries and librarians, and providing feedback to the association. Because of this two-way communication, school librarians have become involved in other Department of Education initiatives and efforts.

Deb is convinced that this relationship with the State Department of Education is of the utmost value in strengthening school library programs in Ohio. She says, "As a profession we worked hard in the face of what seemed to be insurmountable changes by increasing our visibility on state committees and in state activities instead of whining.

Our leadership worked with our membership in providing productive, positive messages about the instructional role provided by a strong school library program" (Logan n. pag.).

In March 2002, due to the changes in the Operating Standards, there was a move to institute major cuts to school libraries in many school districts throughout Ohio. Some interpreted this as the elimination of school librarian positions, but because of the strong, consistent messages about the role of school libraries and librarians in the total instructional program, Dr. Susan Tave Zelman, State Superintendent of Public Instruction said the following in her weekly e-mail message to all school districts:

"A language change regarding school libraries was made in the new Operating Standards for Ohio Schools. The 1983 Minimum Standards required a school library in every school building. The new language requires access to library media programs designed to support student achievement. The language change was not intended to eliminate school libraries; the purpose is to provide flexibility to districts in establishing school library services . . . All students should have access to school library media programs during regular school hours." ("Operating Standards Change Affects School Libraries" n. pag.)

In addition, the Ohio Department of Education's Office of Curriculum and Instruction is in the process of developing Guidelines for Effective School Library Media Programs, which will represent a standards-based approach to school library programs. The project will include three parts: 1) Library Guidelines, which define what students should know and be able to do as a result of an effective school library media program and identify the conditions necessary to establish quality library programs; 2) A Library Toolkit, which provides the evidence-based research that supports the Guidelines and practical examples of implementing them; and 3) The Alignment Guide, which aligns the Library Guidelines with Ohio Academic Content Standards.

OELMA's positive relationship with the Ohio Department of Education has helped to create the kind of awareness that all educators in the state need in order for them to, as Deb puts it, "make your case for you since you are so important to them that they can't do without you. What principals need are kids learning" (Logan n. pag.).

The OELMA Web site <www.oelma.org> presents a press release from May, 2002 that describes the receipt of an $80,000 Library Services and Technology (LSTA) grant, which was awarded through the State Library of Ohio. This grant is being used to produce a video kit to focus on identifying effective Ohio school library media programs that are impacting student learning. Fourteen Ohio school libraries are included in the video as a sampling of effective library media programs. The project, "Student Learning through Ohio School Libraries," is a collaborative effort between OELMA, the Ohio Department of Education, the State Library of Ohio, and INFOhio—the state's K-12 information network.

Besides being used by school districts to identify the characteristics of an effective school library media program, the video kit also provides an excellent advocacy tool that can be used in legislative advocacy efforts on district, state, and national levels.

In states such as Ohio, where the school library association can only use the expertise of a legislative advisor rather than hire a professional lobbyist, building credibility and strong relationships with the state department of education and the state library agency are probably the best avenues for advocacy for school library programs.

Exploring Other Avenues of Support

In some state departments of education, school library services fall under the aegis of Educational Technology. The Wisconsin Department of Public Instruction (DPI) is fortunate to have Neah Lohr as the Director of the Instructional Media and Technology Team. School libraries are under the umbrella of her team. Neah feels that some of the things they are doing in her department are making a difference, even though elementary schools are losing their school librarians as a result of Wisconsin's budget problems. Even in her own office, Neah has lost two library-related consultant positions. But she has not allowed this to dampen her efforts (Lohr n. pag.).

Her department, along with the Wisconsin Educational Media Association (WEMA), planned an Invitational Institute, held at the University of Wisconsin, in November, 2003, which brought together the leadership from Wisconsin's PK-12 school districts: district administrators, curriculum coordinators, district library media directors, district technology coordinators, and university Deans of Education and their faculties, who train Wisconsin's teachers. The Institute was funded by a PT3 (Preparing Tomorrow's Teachers to use Technology) grant to the University of Wisconsin System. The major speakers at the Institute were Ferdi Serim, a board member of the Consortium for School Networking and author of several books on using technology in education, including *Information Technology for Learning: No School Left Behind*, published in 2003; Priscilla Norton from George Mason University, co-author of *Technology in Teaching* (Pearson, Allyn & Bacon, 2000); and Bernie Dodge from San Diego State University, of

WebQuest fame. The breakout sessions at this Institute included the following topics: Big6™, Using Your Data, Scientifically Based Research, and 21st Century Skills. Neah's hope was that after hearing all of the information presented at this Institute these education leaders would see how all of it fits together in a strong, robust library media program in which technology is integrated into all of the information literacy instruction. This realization on the part of education leaders could play an important part in delineating future funding priorities for quality school library staffing and resources.

Often presenting the appropriate information to the appropriate people is a first step in political advocacy for school libraries, since it creates automatic allies who realize the necessity for strong school library programs and who are in positions of leadership to begin to do something about it.

Meanwhile WEMA, along with the Wisconsin Association of School Librarians (WASL), which is a unit of the Wisconsin Library Association (WLA), are working toward restoring the school library consultant positions at the state agency. It is one of the items on WLA's legislative agenda, along with the employment of a certificated librarian in every school, and the maintenance of the Common School Fund income for the purchase of library books and other instructional materials for school libraries.

Donna Steffan is the chair of the WEMA Preparation and Recruitment Committee, a member of the WEMA Executive Committee, and WASL representative on WLA's Library Development and Legislation Committee, and reports that both WASL and WEMA are diligently advocating on behalf of Wisconsin's school library issues. Most WASL members are also members of WEMA, whose membership includes about 80 percent school librarians. Donna says, "Currently, there is a grass roots appeal for building level school librarians to contact the state administration, explaining their critical need for this leadership (at DPI) position" (Steffan n. pag.).

Both school library associations support Wisconsin Legislative Day and National Library Legislative Day. On the state level their goal is to have each team that visits a state legislator's office include a school library representative. Their most critical issue is staffing: keeping their certified school librarians in place at the building and district levels. As in most states grappling with budget cuts, these positions are threatened. The other major issue is maintaining the Common School Fund for school library resources. This fund is attractive to many other programs that want state money, and must be constantly watched by school library advocates. The WLA/WASL and WEMA school library advocates stay in the forefront of these ongoing struggles as they continue to fight for strong school libraries for Wisconsin students.

In May, 2003, Wisconsin sent a team of 13 to Washington, DC for Legislative Day, which included two school librarians and a school district technology coordinator—so almost one fourth of the team was representing school issues. Wisconsin's school library leaders know that political advocacy is essential—especially in today's budget-cutting climate.

Using Technology in School Library Advocacy Efforts

The Internet and the wealth of Web sites it provides has created an excellent tool that can be used in school library advocacy efforts. State and national listservs provide up-to-the-minute information on pending legislation and notices when action is needed. Web sites of state education agencies provide information on standards and curriculum and instruction that can be used in creating issues briefs or message documents to be used as ammunition in all advocacy efforts. The Library Research Service Web site in Colorado and others provide easily printable executive summaries of the school library studies. The Web sites of school library associations provide information for members and others of the association's activities, conferences, and legislative priorities and actions.

School librarians in Pennsylvania are utilizing technology to its utmost benefit in their school library advocacy efforts. Cathi Fuhrman, library department supervisor of the Hempfield, Pennsylvania school district and past chair of the Legislation Committee of the Pennsylvania School Library Association (PSLA) and Lin Carvell, Library Director of the Lancaster County Day School and current chair of the committee have been instrumental in furthering Pennsylvania's advocacy work through the "Legislators @ your library™" Campaign.

Cathi conceived of this innovative campaign in the spring of 1998. She began by writing to the seven state and federal legislators of the district in which her school is situated requesting an 8x10 photograph and a biography for a "Wall of Fame" that she was planning to create in her school library. The responses of all seven were almost immediate, and within a couple of weeks the "Wall of Fame" was up. She pulled books from her shelves that were related—books on government, politics, how a bill becomes a law, the State of Pennsylvania, and Washington, DC to place in a display near the "Wall." She then wrote letters thanking them for their pictures and bios, and included an invitation to them to come and view the wall. Within a short time, five out of the seven had responded, and in a subsequent two-week period, all five visited the library where they could see the wonderful learning environment (enhanced by their "Wall of Fame") for information literacy instruction. The whole idea was just for them to come to see first-hand what a school librarian does each day for students. She also included the district administrators and the district public relations people, and was able to get good coverage in the local newspaper. "It was awesome!" Cathi said. "For me it was so exciting and rejuvenating to be able to 'sell' what the school library does for students" (Fuhrman n. pag.).

Cathi's goal was for every school librarian in Pennsylvania to replicate this activity. In order to accomplish this, she used the PSLA Web site <www.psla.org> where, in the "Legislation" section she created an excellent tool kit that all school librarians could use to organize a "Legislators @ your library™" program in their own schools. With just a couple of "clicks" PSLA members can access the various pieces used in this campaign:

- Effective Ways to Communicate with Legislators
- Guidelines for Contacting Legislators
- Sample Letters to Legislators
- Information for PSLA's regional coordinators to use in replicating the project in their regions
- Sample memos to provide for teachers and school staff before a legislator's visit
- Permission letter to the school administrator requesting his support

In 2002 many Pennsylvania school librarians utilized this excellent packet of materials, and all had positive "Legislators @ your library™" experiences in their own schools. The hope is that this will be an ongoing advocacy activity in Pennsylvania.

Because of the legislators' visits to view their "Wall of Fame" in Cathi's library, she was able to speak with them one-on-one as she showed them around the library. This became a valuable asset when a short time later a detrimental bill arose in the state legislature. Cathi was able to call the state legislators she had already met, and they knew who she was and listened to her opinions regarding the bill. Ultimately, due to statewide advocacy against this bill, it failed. "If every state and federal legislator in the country went to just one school library in their district," says Cathi, "think how powerful that would be" (Fuhrman n. pag.).

Also included in the "Legislation" section of the PSLA Web site are links to the ALA Washington Office and the Pennsylvania School Reform Network (PSRN). At the PSRN site, advocates can find the complete list, alphabetical by topic, of bills affecting public education that have been introduced in the Pennsylvania House and Senate during the current legislative session, along with the opening and closing dates of the session. Again, with a couple of clicks, one can access an individual bill, read the exact text, and learn exactly where that bill is in the legislative process. The site is updated almost daily.

Additionally, on the left-hand side of the PSLA Legislation page, there are immediate links to current state and federal legislative items of interest to school librarians. These might include "Action Needed" messages, titled "ALERT," current news on the status of specific pieces of legislation that affect school libraries, and alerts from ALAWON, the listserv of the ALA Washington Office, which informs listserv members of up-to-the minute action needed or information when bills have been approved (or not) and signed by the President.

PSLA also has a very active school library listserv, which is used by a large majority of its members when issues arise that need immediate action. This was especially true during 2003, when in March the Governor proposed cuts in the state's department of education budget that would seriously undermine the funding of many school library programs. School librarians throughout Pennsylvania contacted the Governor's office to express what these disastrous cuts would do to students' learning.

Listserv POWER!

In 1993 the California School Library Association created a School Library listserv, CALIBK12, as a communication and discussion device, which would bring its members in this geographically large and diverse state closer together. Today CALIBK12 has 1100 subscribers. The listserv has proven to be invaluable as a mechanism used to answer questions, to share stories, and most importantly in this writer's mind, as a powerful political tool. Megan Fuller made this fact most evident in a posting in December 2003. Megan is a library media technician at Aptos Junior High School in California. Aptos is a small town of 9400 residents situated southeast of Santa Cruz on the Monterey Bay. Her post states the following:

"If anybody ever doubted the effectiveness of this list, let it be known that in information there is POWER!

Our district was (is) in financial straits. For the past six weeks I have been using the lessons learned from this list to fight the intended library closures. I have forwarded every letter from Stephen Krashen. I wrote letters quoting all the studies. I asked for and got support from parents and staff. At last night's board meeting ALL of our district's libraries were saved! Today I got an e-mail from the Superintendent thanking me for my professionalism.

I want to thank all of you who subscribe to this list. You are a tremendous support. My program is better for my belonging to this list. Thank you Barbara and Martha (California's school library consultants in the California Department of Education) for all the information you give us and for the work you do at the State" (Fuller, "Library Closures" n. pag.).

Megan's message engendered an avalanche of responses asking her to tell the story of exactly what she did to turn a dismal situation around. Within a day she posted her story on the listserv. The story is presented in her own words below:

"About six weeks ago school sites were notified that the district was going to have to cut $9 million from its budget for the 04/05 year and an additional million for 05/06. The district's budget committee had brainstormed areas that could be cut. It seems that closing the 28 libraries and laying off library personnel could save $900,000. (I never was clear how they came up with that amount.) The budget committee then sent a list of all the proposed cuts to the school sites with instructions that we were to prioritize the list. The amount attached to libraries was one of the largest figures, with transportation being the largest proposed cut. Of course the Arts, Music, and Sports were also included on the list. Everyone at my site was absolutely horrified to see libraries on the list.

It was proposed by our school's counselor (whose position was also on the cut list) that the entire staff should make a trip to the next budget meeting and voice our opinions; so about 80 percent of our staff attended the meeting. You should have seen the look on the committee's faces when we all arrived. We were very polite, but I think it disturbed the powers that be to see [such a large] group show up. Anyway, at that meeting I asked how they had come up with the list. I was told that everyone on the committee had brainstormed ideas. That there was, 'no such thing as a bad idea.' Then they put everything on the list and it was done—flawed research process. I asked had they done any further research on their ideas? No. When I asked if they knew that our libraries actually make money for the district, the committee was unaware of that fact. So I spoke about the $65,000 in grants that I had successfully been awarded for 'Reading is Fundamental,' a district-wide program that is a collaboration with the public library and 13 of our district's school libraries, plus a Head Start program. I spoke about fundraising efforts that I was aware of at other sites, such as book fairs and pencil sales. I also spoke about the state money and how hard the district's library committee had worked to make a plan so that the state money would be available to our district. I also spoke about how for the past two years our libraries did not get that money and that it was rolled over into the general fund. (I did get a little hot under the collar there, and I do not recommend that!) A member of the Board of Trustees sits as a member of the budget committee and she suggested that any further comments should be e-mailed to the board.

The next morning I began working on a letter to be e-mailed to the board. It took me several days to come up with an excellent letter making all the appropriate arguments as to why it was a bad idea to cut libraries. This is where I used all the quotes, statistics, and attached [information from the studies of] Keith Curry Lance. I talked about textbook loss; I quoted [a] Seattle news article regarding the drop in reading/writing scores. My friend, the grammar teacher [at my school] helped me edit the letter and made me take out all the pissy [sic] stuff. I sent that e-mail to every librarian in the district, every board member, the Superintendent, and all five of the Assistant Superintendents (who, by the way, were NOT on the cut list), plus my principal and the staff at my school. Because I had created a nice big 'contacts' list, all replies, kudos and comments, of which there were many, were sent back and forth as 'Reply All.' Several teachers from my site also wrote letters, including one PE teacher who said sports should be cut before libraries. Made me tear up, you bet.

I was dismayed when the board began replying to the letter, 'There are no sacred cows!' I was sure I was going to be job-hunting in the near future. Only the president of the board said that she would keep my arguments in mind, giving me a ray of hope.

Meanwhile, back at school, I began preparing my students for the idea that there might not be a library next year. This really shocked the students. Two industrious young ladies decided to write a petition. They got just about every kid to sign it (lots of junior high aside comments included).

As I went out into the community I spoke to everyone I met, 'Have you heard they are planning to close school libraries?' Conversations standing in line at the bank and at restaurants. 'Write a letter, call the board, and let me give you some contact information.' I ran into one old friend from my 'Odyssey of the Mind' days who is a lawyer and asked him to speak at the next board meeting.

At the next board meeting, I made it a point to speak. Is it only my district that puts the really tough stuff off until the very end of the board meetings, or is this a well-known tactic? My good friend who is the Secretary for the Friends of the Watsonville Library and I waited until nearly 11:30 p.m. to be heard. Let me tell you I was going to be so eloquent . . . around 10:00 my brain turned off, so I think I said something like, 'UBBA, UBBA, don't close libraries.' Actually, I spoke about the Superintendent's two new programs, the Million Word Challenge and the Book of the Month, and how even though the programs were instituted without notifying the librarians, we were excited about the challenges and were running with them. (At Aptos Junior High we have three students at over a million words already, and about 75 percent of the student body is on track to be at a million words by June.) My friend spoke about how the public library was not prepared to service the entire needs of the district's students. The president of our union spoke about how foolish it was to close libraries.

Back at school I held a 'Mission Impossible' day. AJHS had 104 students who had not read anything all year. So I made little cute invitations, barcoded so that the kids couldn't use the 'I forgot my ID' excuse. I pulled every guaranteed kid-pleasing (short) book off the shelf and set them out on the tables so the kids couldn't get lost in the shelves. I played the 'Mission Impossible' theme and dressed up in sunglasses and a trench coat. I got books into the hands of 101 of the hardcore non-readers that day. Then I e-mailed my huge contact list and told them about what a great day it had been. I do not usually toot my own horn, but call me Gabriel these days. I got the other librarians to talk about what was going on in their libraries too. I forwarded all of Stephen Krashen's wonderful letters as well.

Finally, December 3rd arrived. Four groups presented their prioritized cut lists to the board: Administrators, Certificated, Classified, and Parents. Libraries did not show up on three of the four lists" (Fuller, "What worked for me" n. pag.).

The result, as quoted above in Megan's exultant original post, is that the cuts were subverted, the positions were maintained, and the libraries were kept open. Her original post again exemplifies the strength and power that a statewide school library listserv can wield in advocacy efforts.

State Association Support for Legislative Days

Participation in state and national Library Legislative Days varies from state to state. Some states do not even have them, and others do, but with limited involvement of school library people. In many states the state library association, which often organizes Legislative Day activities, is often most concerned with public libraries, and school library issues may not even be addressed at all. In other states, the school library association is a section or a special interest group under the umbrella of the state library association, and school library issues may be ignored altogether.

In Texas, the members of the Texas Association of School Librarians (TASL) are equal partners with their Texas Library Association (TLA) colleagues. Janice Richardson, TASL president, explains that TASL is a division of TLA, and says, "Overall, I personally feel that we get good support from the association. This past year (2003) when the legislature was cutting funds left and right, TLA was fighting incredibly hard to support school issues" (Richardson n. pag.).

TLA's legislative agenda has included support for school library issues for the past several years, and in 1999 school library appropriations dominated. Since funding for school library materials depended 100 percent on the whims of the local school board, it was evident that state support was necessary in order to bring some sense of equity for Texas students in terms of per-pupil funding as well as items per pupil as delineated by *School Library Programs: Standards and Guidelines for Texas.*

Texas has a unique state legislature, which only sits in session every other year. They convene in January of odd-numbered years, and bills must be passed and signed by the Governor by mid-June. In the 1999 session, the 76th Texas Legislature established a precedent. For the first time in the state's history they passed funding for school library materials: 25 cents per student, an appropriation made in the form of a rider to the Texas Education Agency budget. Although this figure seems like "small change," it made a telling difference in Texas school libraries. TASL devoted all of its legislative efforts to this campaign, and school librarians joined hundreds of Texas library advocates as they trooped to Austin, their capital, for TLA Legislative Day in February, 1999. Also passed in this 76th Legislature was funding for a pay raise for school librarians.

In the 77th Texas Legislature of 2001, again because of participation of Texas school librarians and their supporters in Legislative Day, the appropriation was increased to 30 cents per student. But the need for additional support still existed, and TLA/TASL's plan for the 78th Texas Legislature, which would convene in January 2003, was a campaign for $1.00 per student for school library materials. A valuable asset to this campaign was the landmark study, *Texas School Libraries, Standards, Resources, Services and Students' Performance*, which demonstrated higher performance on the Texas Assessment of Academic Skills (TAAS) in schools with librarians than in schools without librarians. This provided an excellent piece of ammunition for Texas school librarians and their supporters to use at Legislative Day in February 2003. A unique element of this Legislative Day was the participation of the Texas Professional Association for Library Sales (TPALS), the vendors who supply all Texas libraries with print and non-print materials. The inclusion of library vendors was another positive move in TLA/TASL's legislative agenda, and proved to be an excellent idea.

TASL also realizes the necessity of having its members involved in advocacy on the national level, and the association subsidizes two members to attend National Library Legislative Day in Washington, DC. Other TASL members choose to attend on their own to advocate for school library issues with their Texas members of congress.

School library associations have a very crucial role to play in political advocacy efforts. Strong legislative committees are a must since they can stay "on top of" the issues and keep their membership informed, and support for state and national Library Legislative Days encourages members to become involved in garnering support for their libraries on all levels.

A Special Event

Organizing a Legislative Day in the District has been discussed in Chapter 5, but here is another approach to creating a positive awareness on the part of legislators of school libraries and librarians and what they do.

Judi Moreillon is a librarian at Sabino High School in Tucson, Arizona, an adjunct assistant professor in the Department of Language, Reading, and Culture at the University of Arizona, and the Chair of the Teacher-Librarian Division (TLD) of the Arizona Library Association (AzLA). For two consecutive years, TLD representatives and the AzLA Legislative Committee have been responsible for spearheading a legislative campaign for a bill to require at least one full-time librarian in every K-12 public school in Arizona.

In 2004, these creative Arizona school librarians launched a campaign to save Arizona's public school libraries. They staged an advocacy event entitled "No School Left Behind @ your library™." The half-day event was a tour of school libraries in the Tucson area, with librarians acting as chauffeurs, using their own personal cars to transport the guests to the individual schools. The goals of this special day to increase awareness of school libraries were as follows:

- To spotlight the contributions school library programs with full-time professional teacher-librarians make to student achievement;
- To compare and contrast library resources—human and material—in urban and rural schools/districts;
- To understand the critical role of school libraries/librarians in meeting the goals of No Child Left Behind;
- To prepare for the 2004 legislative session with regard to bills affecting school libraries: full time teacher-librarians in every K-12 public school in Arizona, teacher-librarians counted by the Auditor General's office as "instructional" rather than "administrative," and full funding for library materials budgets (Moreillon n. pag.).

Judi and her TLD colleagues invited a group of leaders from Arizona's state legislature to join school librarians on this tour. Other invitees included the editor/reporters from the *Arizona Daily Star*, representatives from the Governor's office and the state department of education, and members of the Citizen Budget Review Committee. The plan was to give the school librarian "chauffeurs" a perfect opportunity to answer questions and speak from personal experience about their work with students, teachers, and school communities as they drove guests to the school library sites on the tour. Another unique part of this day's activity was a virtual tour of five school libraries in Douglas, Arizona, which is one hundred miles southeast of Tucson on the Mexican border. Douglas is a small town whose school district serves the surrounding rural area as well. The virtual tour was accomplished through a PowerPoint presentation at the end of the half-day car tour.

The committee also sent a letter explaining the tour to 30 local educators, politicians, and civic leaders, asking them to support this initiative of the Campaign to Save Arizona's School Libraries by lending their names to a list that would be included on the requests to principals to visit their schools and on the invitations to legislators and other decision makers. A form was provided for them to sign indicating their agreement to be a sponsor of this event.

Each guest was provided with a binder that included the relevant research that demonstrates the connection between strong school library programs and increased student achievement, including the studies done by Lance and Krashen, excerpts from neighboring New Mexico's *How School Libraries Improve Outcomes for Children*, the proceedings from the June, 2002 White House Conference on School Libraries, and statistics on the per-student expenditure on school library materials by the individual school districts in Arizona. In addition, each vehicle had a photo album showing students and teachers engaged in library-centered learning experiences.

The tour began at Ventana Vista School Library, which is fully supported/fully funded and employs a full-time professional librarian. After greetings and breakfast, guests traveled to three other elementary schools and a high school. All the schools were within a half-hour of the starting point at Ventana Vista. Two of the library programs were struggling with part-time professionals and one had no professional at all. All the vehicles traveled the same route and the participants toured the school libraries as a team. Visits at each library lasted from ten minutes (where the library was closed because there was no professional scheduled for that day) to thirty minutes (where a fully-collaborative professional librarian was working with students and teachers in a fully-integrated program.) Participants returned to Ventana Vista's library for snacks and the virtual tour of the Douglas school libraries, some of which are simply rooms with disorganized, dog-eared paperback books. The virtual tour was followed by a question and answer session.

Judi described Arizona's school library situation as follows:

"At present, the pattern is for large urban school districts to employ full-time professionals in school libraries; smaller urban districts and rural districts to employ part-time professionals (serving as many as five schools), paraprofessionals, and/or volunteers at the elementary and middle school levels. In recent months, even urban schools with site-based budget control and shrinking budgets have opted to eliminate professionals in their school libraries."

She further states, "At least in Arizona, it is only by mandating full-time professional teacher-librarians through legislation that we can ensure the future of our profession and the right of Arizona students and teachers to an information literate education" (Moreillon n. pag.).

The "No School Left Behind @ your library™" tour provided a vehicle through which to build a solid base of support among Tucson and Arizona community leaders. The information provided for them in their binders as well as the actual opportunity to see school libraries and librarians "in action" created the awareness that would influence their work in the state legislature and in the media. TLD members and the AzLA Legislative Committee were able to use the connections made on this special day as they continued their advocacy efforts for full staffing and full funding of school libraries when the next legislative session began. Again, by being proactive, creative, passionate, and committed, Arizona school librarians made a difference.

Relationships Count!

Carolyn Giambra is a retired library media specialist and was the district instructional specialist in charge of school libraries for the Williamsville Central School District in Williamsville, New York. She is also a past-president of the New York Library Association with many years of experience in library advocacy efforts. From her experiences Carolyn has learned of the importance of knowing legislators well and forging personal relationships with them.

During her working years she had made several visits to the office of the assemblyman who represented her school district as a part of the New York Library Association's Lobby/Library Day. The assemblyman had expressed support for schools and had also mentioned that he had once been a Social Studies teacher. One year the superintendent of schools of the Williamsville school district was contacted by the assemblyman's office requesting suggestions for the expenditure of $20,000, which would be funded as the assemblyman's "member item," in essence a gift to the district. Each of the ten instructional specialists of the district was asked to place two items on the list, thus providing the assemblyman with 20 items from which to choose. The requestors were not identified.

Carolyn placed the following two items on the list: New ADA-compliant signage for each of the district's 13 libraries @ $300 each ($3900) and new "light up" globes for each library @ $800 each ($10,400). "Both of my items were selected!" Carolyn says.

"So the libraries received $14,300 of the $20,000" (Giambra n. pag.).

The assemblymember's office subsequently had a photograph published in the local newspaper featuring several students showing the assemblymember a spot on the "lit up" globe, with one of the new library signs showing in the background.

When Carolyn was deciding on which items to place on the request list, she took into consideration several political realities that she had learned from her many years of advocacy activities. She chose to mention "ADA-compliant" in her request since this was a politically correct term at the time. She also appealed to the assemblyman's agenda, relating to the fact that he had been a Social Studies teacher. She provided a photo opportunity for the assemblyman with students after the materials had been received.

Carolyn's experience shows once again that establishing ongoing contacts with legislators, knowing what interests them, and using this information whenever necessary can lead to success for school libraries.

Whatever Works—Try It!

The purpose of the success stories in this chapter, and, in fact, this entire book, is to let readers know that you have the power to create change for your school libraries. The various scenarios from the 11 featured states show one thing: school library advocates are determined, energetic, industrious, creative, and passionate. These leaders of our profession, using a variety of techniques, tools, and methodologies, are making a difference for students all over these United States.

Perhaps you have read something that tickled your fancy—something that made you think, "Wow! That sounds like fun!" or "Gee, I could do that!" Your libraries need it. Your students need it. There is only one answer left: You have the power! Use it!

Appendix A

The "Always" List:
Ten Tips to Remember

I.   ALWAYS BE HONEST
- No exaggeration or embellishment of facts
- Quote figures that are accurate

II.   ALWAYS BE COURTEOUS
- Offer to help elected officials
- If you disagree with their point of view, explain consequences to students
- Do not threaten with "I will see that no one votes for you."

III.   ALWAYS COMMUNICATE/COMMUNICATE/COMMUNICATE
- Respond quickly to requests for information
- Provide straight information: do your homework and be aware of the opposition
- Visit legislators early with your list of issues and information
- Prepare a one-page fact sheet related to your issues

IV.   ALWAYS REFRAIN FROM CRITICIZING OTHER LEGISLATORS
- Concentrate only on the legislator with whom you are meeting
- Your "enemy" may be their friend

V.   ALWAYS BE IMPORTANT TO LEGISLATORS
- Become known as the "expert" on school libraries who can provide information
- Relate with their staff also; they can be very helpful

VI. ALWAYS BE SWIFT
- Be bright/be brief/be gone!

VII. ALWAYS BE UNDERSTANDING
- Know their background/culture/politics
- Patience is a virtue
- Be able to compromise

VIII. ALWAYS OFFER ASSISTANCE & BUILD COALITIONS
- Educate others in the community
- Let all know how a strong school library helps them

IX. ALWAYS BE A CHEERLEADER
- Thank-you letters are essential
- Even after a "wrong" vote, thank officials for taking time with you

X. ALWAYS DISPLAY PROFESSIONALISM
- Do not be "uppity"
- Be confident and maintain a sense of humor

Appendix B

What You Should Know About Your Legislator

- How were they elected? By what margin?
- What were their campaign promises?
- Who endorsed them?
- Which other officials do they relate with?
- What do they like/dislike?
- What is the ethnic/economic/business makeup of their district?
- Who were their campaign donors?
- Which community groups are they connected with? (Elks/Lions/PTA, etc.)
- Which issues concern them the most?
- What leadership positions do they hold in the legislature/board of education?

Being an Effective Advocate with Legislators

- Money is not the only issue
- Find ways to include school libraries in other pieces of legislation
- Maintain good will/build relationships
- Deliver what you promise
- Create/build understanding of what your library program is about
- Be brief/specific/informative/courteous/firm
- Be appreciative

Appendix C

Be an
Effective Speaker

- Be prepared, know your audience's perspective
- Personalize your message, make it important to them
- Write out your speech/notes, but talk, do not read
- Use anecdotes; tell stories
- Use visual aids where possible
- Be brief, but be sure to reiterate your main issue at least three times
- Be understood; do not try to impress; do not use library lingo
- Present a "Call to Action": three key points stating what you want them to do
- Distribute handouts after you talk to insure listening
- Invite/anticipate questions, and be prepared with answers; offer to find answers you do not know
- Be passionate
- Thank/thank/thank

When the Media Calls

- Ask questions/figure out their angle
- Be prepared/be clear/be accurate
- Watch out for manipulation
- Use short, punchy quotes
- Think first/talk second
- Do not be afraid to pause
- Use an "open face"/smile

Appendix D

Helpful Web Sites for Advocacy

AASL ADVOCACY TOOLKIT <www.ala.org>

In the "Search" field, enter "AASL Advocacy Toolkit"

AASL POSITION STATEMENTS <www.ala.org>

In the "Search" field, enter "AASL Position Statements"

ALA LEGISLATIVE ACTION CENTER <www.ala.org/washoff>

Communicate with your U.S. congress members and senators via e-mail.

ALA RESOLUTION ON SCHOOL LIBRARIES <www.ala.org/aasl/>

Click on "Issues and Advocacy" tab at top of page; then click on "Advocacy" on next page.

ALA RESOURCES FOR LIBRARY ADVOCATES <www.ala.org/pio>

Click on "Advocacy" for links to a variety of resources advocates can use, the best of which are "The Library Advocate's Handbook" and "A Library Advocate's Guide to Building Information Literate Communities." These can be accessed by scrolling down and clicking on "Advocacy Publications" under "Other Resources."

ALA WASHINGTON OFFICE NEWSLINE (ALAWON) <www.ala.org/washoff/alawon>

A free, e-mail publication providing urgent and late-breaking news from Washington, DC.

"LEGISLATORS @ YOUR LIBRARY™" CAMPAIGN <www.psla.org/association/committee/legislation/legislation.php3>

Provides all of the links to the packet for this advocacy program in Pennsylvania.

MEDIA TRAINING <www.lustberg.net>

Provides Arch Lustberg's techniques for speaking before boards, committees, etc.

OHIO STATE SUPERINTENDENT OF PUBLIC INSTRUCTION, STATEMENT ON SCHOOL LIBRARIES (May, 2002) <www.ode.state.oh.us/superintendent/email/2002/05-31-02.asp>

Presents the entire statement referenced in Chapter 6.

SCHOOL LIBRARIES ON THE WEB <www.sldirectory.com/libsf/stlibs.html>

Click on "United States" or any other country for a wealth of links to school library information.

SCHOOL LIBRARIES—HISTORY <http://falcom.jmu.edu~ramseyil/libhistory.htm>

Provides information and links on important dates and documents related to the history of school libraries.

SCHOOL LIBRARIES—NEWS AND ARTICLES <http://libraries.surfwax.com/files/School_Libraries.html>

Provides current articles about school libraries from publications around the world.

SCHOOL LIBRARY STUDIES <www.lrs.org>

> Library Research Service, Colorado State Library presents links to the studies done by Keith Curry Lance, et al.

"STATE CONTENT STANDARDS: A 50-STATE RESOURCE"
<www.ccsso.org/content/pdfs/StateContentStandards.pdf>

> Compiled by the Council of Chief State School Officers; lists content standards for each state with links to state departments of education. Can be used to look at the eight states which have Library Standards, or used as a resource in creating standards for your state.

WHITE HOUSE CONFERENCE ON SCHOOL LIBRARIES
<www.imls.gov/pubs/whitehouse0602/whitehouse.htm>

> Presents the full proceedings of this landmark conference sponsored by First Lady Laura Bush on June 4, 2002.

Appendix E

Prototype Bargaining Language – Library Media Center Certificated Librarian

Section—Library/Media Center Standards and Guidelines

.1 Staffing

A. All library media centers will be staffed by qualified library media specialist(s). The minimum qualification is certification and library endorsement or equivalent at both elementary and secondary level.

B. Schools shall have a library staffed by a qualified library media specialist (as defined above).

C. Minimum FTE Staffing Ratio: Library Media Specialists and Library Classified Support Staff:

> # of students enrolled FTE Library Media Specialists FTE Library Classified
>
> Up to 600 1.0 1.0
> 601-1000 1.5 1.5
> 1000 & up 2.0 2.5

D. When an elementary library program exceeds twenty-one (21) classes per week, the librarian will receive an additional half hour of library clerical time per day. This shall include all grade levels, including Kindergarten.

E. The library media specialist at the secondary level will hold Department Head status as per provisions of the contract.

F. Class-size lids apply for Library Media Specialists.

.2 Workday

A. The workday for the library media specialist shall be the same as any full time teacher in the building. The decision to have extended hours will be scheduled in cooperation with the library media specialist. Library media specialists will receive the same amount of planning time as any other certificated staff member.

.3 Extended Contracts

A. To support and develop the services of the instructional media program to best serve the school district, the library media specialist shall have an extended contract of a minimum, but not limited to, ten (10) days. These additional days shall occur on a schedule mutually determined by the employee and the immediate supervisor.

B. Additional extended contracts or supplemental extracurricular days will be contracted at per diem or 1/180 of basic contract, whichever is greater.

.4 Budget/Instructional Materials

The total library media program budget will be a minimum of the number of students per building times two times the current average replacement cost per item.

.5 Facilities

All planning of new facilities or remodeling of existing facilities will include the library staff that is using the facility.

.6 Training

Library media specialists will meet during the school workday for two (2) hours every month for district-wide meetings to coordinate programs and exchange best practices.

.7 Library Bill of Rights

From: *Information Power* for Washington State 1991.
> (If this is not included in the master Agreement, it should be part of District policy and referenced in the contract. Reference ALA Library Bill of Rights and Right To Read.)

"The American Library Association affirms that all libraries are forums for information and ideas and that the following basic policies should guide their services.

A. Books and other library resources should be provided for the interest, information, and enlightenment of all people of the community the library serves. Materials should not be excluded because of the origin, background, or views of those contributing to their creation.

B. Libraries should provide materials and information presenting all points of view on current and historical issues. Materials should not be proscribed or removed because of partisan and doctrinal disapproval.

C. Libraries should challenge censorship in the fulfillment of their responsibility to provide information and enlightenment.

D. Libraries should cooperate with all persons and groups concerned with resisting abridgment of free expression and free access to ideas.

E. A person's right to use a library should not be denied or abridged because of origin, age, background, or views.

F. Libraries which make exhibit spaces and meeting rooms available to the public they serve should make such facilities available on an equitable basis, regardless of the beliefs or affiliations of individuals or groups requesting their use."

(Used with permission of Marie-Anne Harkness and WEMA.)

Appendix F

NCLIS Statement on School Librarians

June 4, 2002

SCHOOL LIBRARIES:
KNOWLEDGE NAVIGATORS THROUGH TROUBLED TIMES

Today's White House Conference on School Libraries, hosted by First Lady Laura Bush, demonstrates the commitment of this Administration to improving education and its recognition that school libraries play a major role in student achievement.

The Members of the National Commission on Libraries and Information Science share this commitment. Last year, the Commission held a hearing in Cincinnati to learn firsthand how the explosion of information technology has affected the work and status of school libraries and school librarians and how school libraries and school librarians are affecting student achievement. The full report on the Hearing will be available shortly. The key findings are summarized below.

1. Studies in Alaska, Colorado, Kentucky, Massachusetts, Oregon, Pennsylvania, and Texas provide empirical proof that students have a higher level of academic achievement in schools with strong school libraries staffed with professional school librarians.

2. Reports indicate that school library funding for staff and materials is being dramatically cut back due to limited fiscal resources in

many school districts. Far too many schools lack a full-time school librarian and many elementary school libraries are staffed by volunteers and may only be open one to two days a week. For example, during the 1999-2000 school year, only one California school in seven had a credentialed library media specialist on campus part-time or more.

3. The rapid growth of technology for use in schools has had a negative impact on school libraries, as funds for support of school library collections have been diverted to paying for hardware, software, and telecommunications.

4. The school library is a place where students can learn the basics of inquiry and become information literate. This is a critical lifetime skill that prepares students to recognize when information is needed and to locate, evaluate, and use effectively the relevant information. This skill is made more critical by the proliferation of information, misinformation, and opinion on the Internet.

5. School librarians must be involved in a leadership role in making the delivery of the curriculum an active inquiring model using both print and digitized resources. When school librarians participate on curriculum and standards committees, their collaboration with classroom teachers enhances learning opportunities for students.

6. Where site-based management has transferred decision-making to individual schools, libraries will flourish only when the Principal understands the importance of the library and the need for a trained school librarian. Too often, the library and the librarian/media specialist are competing for resources with other "enrichment" activities such as art and music. A well-equipped and well-staffed school library should be a necessity for every school, not an optional program.

7. The lack of adequate funding for school libraries and the absence of standards that recognize the need for professional school librarians have widened the learning gap between students in affluent schools and those from at-risk schools. Increasingly, parents and parent-teacher associations feel obliged to raise private funds to support school library collections, and even to pay for staffing, because of inadequate public funding. In schools that do not have the ability to augment public funds, students are left without the benefit of a good school library.

8. Too many school libraries today have books with average copyright dates 20 to 30 years old, thereby useless for curriculum support. Too many schools only have the ability to provide 15 minutes to a half-hour a week per student for either computer instruction or research.

The National Commission believes that school libraries are the heart and soul of the education process. The significance of the school librarian as "gatekeeper" to information in all formats is profound. Without adequate school libraries, and well-trained librarians to manage, organize, and facilitate information access for students, without school librarians who are effective partners in the learning process, without school librarians who are actively involved in building the information literacy of students and of teachers, our future generations will be denied the skills to help them become productive and well informed citizens.

The President of the United States is clearly committed to improving education and literacy. He has called reading the "new civil right." For the first time in history, there is a librarian—indeed, a school librarian—as First Lady of this Nation.

The National Commission on Libraries and Information Science looks forward to working with the Administration and the Congress to improve school libraries and, through them, student achievement. The Commission believes that improved school libraries will ensure, in the words of President Bush, that no child is left behind.

– – –

The National Commission on Libraries and Information Science is a permanent, independent agency of the Federal government charged by Public Law 91-345 to appraise the adequacies and deficiencies of current library and information resources and services and to advise the President and Congress on national and international library and information policies and plans.

Works Cited

"About SLMR." *American Library Association*. 22 Mar. 2004.
  <www.ala.org>

"ALA Washington Office." *American Library Association*. 8 June 2003.
  <www.ala.org/washoff>

Angelou, Maya. Interview with Dan Rather. *CBS Evening News with Dan Rather*. CBS. KCBS, Los Angeles. 28 Aug. 2003.

Anonymous. "KC Info." E-mail to the author. 22 Sept. 2003.

"Current Legislation and Regulation Issues for School Libraries."
  Kansas Association of School Librarians. 11 May 2003.
  <www.cgrove417.org/cghs/KASL.leg.html>

Fuhrman, Cathi. "Legislators@ your Library™." E-mail to the author. 22 Sept. 2003.

Fuhrman, Cathi. Telephone interview. 24 Sept. 2003.

Fuller, Megan. "Library Closures." Online posting. 04 Dec. 2003.
  CALIBK12.

Fuller, Megan. "What worked for me." Online posting. 05 Dec. 2003.
  CALIBK12.

"General Membership Meeting – April 18, 2002." *New Mexico Library Association*. 10 May 2003. <www.nmla.org/minutes/041802.html>

Giambra, Carolyn. "Advocacy Story." E-mail to the author. 7 Oct. 2003.

Hargett, Debbie. "Success Story." E-mail to the author. 1 June 2003.

Harkness, Marie-Anne. "RE: school library advocacy." E-mail to the author. 23 Sept. 2003.

"Hearings on School Libraries." *National Commission on Libraries and Information Science*. 23 Mar. 2004. <www.nclis.gov/news/2001minutes/April-2001-trans.pdf>

"House Bill 434." *Maryland General Assembly*. 15 May 2003. <http://mlis.state.md.us/2001rs/bills/hb/hb034.rtf>

"The Impact of State Funding for Libraries." *Colorado Department of Education*. 02 Jan. 2004. <www.cde.state.co.us/cdelib/download/pdf/LibraryImpact/pdf>

"Improving School Libraries and Independent Reading." *University of Evansville*. 02 Jan. 2004. <www.evansville.edu/mgrnweb/inreading2002.htm>

Johnson, Doug. "Budget cuts." Online posting. 24 Dec. 2002. *AASLFORUM*.

Krashen, Stephen. Notes from conference presentation. *California School Library Association/Southern Section*. Ventura, CA. Mar. 1994.

Krashen, Stephen. *The Power of Reading*. Englewood, CO: Libraries Unlimited, 1993.

Lance, Keith Curry. *How School Librarians Help Kids Achieve Standards*. San Jose, CA: Hi Willow, 2000.

Lance, Keith Curry. *The Impact of School Library Media Centers on Academic Achievement*. Denver: Colorado Department of Education, 1992.

Lance, Keith Curry. *Information Empowered*. Juneau: Alaska State Library, 2000.

Lance, Keith Curry. *Powering Achievement: School Library Programs Make a Difference – the evidence*. San Jose, CA: Hi Willow, 2001.

"Legislation." *California School Library Association*. 06 May 2003. <www.schoolibrary.org>

"Legislation." *Massachusetts School Library Media Association*. 01 May 2003. <www.mslma.org/legislation/legislationfactsheet01.html>

"Legislative Issues." *Iowa Educational Media Association*. 10 May 2003. <www.iema-ia.org/IEMA275.html>

"The Libraries of South Carolina." *University of South Carolina – School of Library and Information Science*. 08 May 2003. <www.libsci.sc.edu/histories/public/frayser/fray18.html>

Logan, Deb. Telephone interview. 21 Sept. 2003.

Lohr, Neah. "RE: school library advocacy." E-mail to the author. 25 Sept. 2003.

Lustberg, Arch. *How to Sell Yourself: Winning Techniques for Selling Yourself . . . Your Ideas . . . Your Message*. Franklin Lakes, NJ: Career Press, 2002.

Lustberg, Arch. "March 2003 Speaker Tip." *Arch Lustberg Communications*. 4 Jan. 2004. <www.lustberg.net/archives.htm#MARCH%202003%20SPEAKER%20TIP>

Lustberg, Arch. Notes from conference presentation. *California Association of Library Trustees and Commissioners*. Sacramento, CA. 2 Feb. 2002.

Moreillon, Judi. "No School Left Behind @ your library™." E-mail to the author. 23 Sept. 2003.

O'Neill, Tip. *All Politics Is Local*. Avon, MA: Adams Media, 1994.

"Operating Standards Change Affects School Libraries." *Ohio Department of Education*. 21 Sept. 2003. <www.ode.state.oh.us/ Curriculum-Assessment/school_library>

"Politics." *Webster's New World College Dictionary, Fourth Edition*. New York: Macmillan USA, 1997.

"Prototype Bargaining Language – Library Media Center Certificated Librarian." *Washington Library Media Association*. 23 Sept. 2003. <www.wlma.org/Professional/bargaining.htm>

Richardson, Janice. "School Library Advocacy." E-mail to the author. 24 Sept. 2003.

Sheketoff, Emily. Telephone interview. 17 Sept. 2003.

Steffan, Donna. "RE: WISCONSIN." E-mail to the author. 26 Sept. 2003.

Sudakow, Roslyn. Telephone interview. 10 Sept. 2003.

"Texas Library Association – Legislative Program Overview." *Texas Library Association*. 7 June 2003. <www.txla.org/htm/legis/ leg_over.html>

Further Reading

Boyers, Sara Jane. *Teen Power Politics: Make Yourself Heard.* Brookfield, CT: Millbrook, 2000.

Carville, James and Paul Begala. *Buck Up, Suck Up, and Come Back when You Foul Up.* New York: Simon, 2002.

Dellums, Ronald V. *Lying Down with the Lions: A Public Life from the Streets of Oakland to the Halls of Power.* Boston: Beacon, 2000.

Flowers, Helen F. *Public Relations for School Library Media Programs.* New York: Neal-Schumann, 1998.

Gillmor, Dan. "Putting On a Powerful Presentation." *Hemispheres.* Mar., 1996: 31-34.

Gladwell, Malcolm. *The Tipping Point: How Little Things Can Make a Big Difference.* Boston: Little, 2000.

Halsey, Richard S. *Lobbying for Public and School Libraries: A History and Political Playbook.* Lanham, MD: Scarecrow, 2003.

Hartzell, Gary. "Sharing Your Expertise." *School Library Journal.* July 2003: 39.

Hutchinson, Carol-Anne. "Working with Your School Board." *Teacher Librarian.* April, 2002: 58-59.

Jamieson, Kathleen Hall. *Everything You Think You Know About Politics . . . And Why You're Wrong.* Boulder: Perseus, 2000.

"Message-based vs. Relationship-based Grass Roots Strategies." *Soapbox Consulting*. 7 June 2003. <www.soapboxconsulting.com/svcsgrassvs.htm>

Newbigging, William. "A Few Observations on the History of Successful Lobbying." *Ontario Confederation of University Faculty Associations*. 18 July 2003. <www.ocufa.on.ca/forum/spring99/lobbying.asp>

Reed, Sally Gardner. *Making the Case for Your Library*. New York: Neal-Schumann, 2001.

Shaw, Randy. *The Activists Handbook*. Berkelely: University of California Press, 1996.

Turner, Anne M. *Getting political: An action guide for librarians*. New York: Neal-Schumann, 1997.

Index

About the Author

Sandy Schuckett is a retired library media teacher who worked for 38 years in elementary and middle school libraries in the Los Angeles Unified School District. She is the Vice President Emerita for Legislation of the California School Library Association, and a former chair of the Legislation Committee of the American Association of School Librarians. She has been an activist in advocating for school libraries in the local, state, and national arenas for more than twenty-five years.

Sandy is a frequent conference presenter on issues dealing with school library advocacy, multilingual library book collection development, training parents to read to young children, and diversity in the school library profession. She was also the editor of the "Governmental Relations" column for the California School Library Association Newsletter for ten years. In "real life" Sandy's interests include reading, cooking, eating in interesting restaurants, attending live theatre, listening to jazz, and watching old movies on TV.

www.ingramcontent.com/pod-product-compliance
Ingram Content Group UK Ltd.
Pitfield, Milton Keynes, MK11 3LW, UK
UKHW031249020325
455689UK00008B/160